edit
illus

A
MUCH-MALIGNED
TOWN
Opinions of Reading
1126-2008

Other books by Adam Sowan published by Two Rivers Press:

Abattoirs Road to Zinzan Street: Reading's Streets and their Names
The Holy Brook, or, The Granator's Tale
A Mark of Affection: the Soane Obelisk in Reading
The Stranger in Reading

First published in the UK in 1997; 2nd edition published in 2008 by
Two Rivers Press
35–39 London Street
Reading RG1 4PS
www.tworiverspress.com

Two Rivers Press is a member of Inpress

Designed by Nadja Guggi

Printed and bound by Antony Rowe Ltd., Chippenham

ISBN 978-1-901677-61-4

Two Rivers Press gratefully acknowledges
financial assistance from Reading Borough Council

PREFACE TO THE SECOND EDITION

In the ten years since this book first appeared I have stumbled upon a lot more printable opinions, stretching its coverage from 411 to 882 years. I have deleted one complete entry, Jonathan Meades's long piece based on a short visit circa 1989; shortened the extracts from John Man's *The Stranger in Reading*, because the whole book is now available in my new annotated edition from Two Rivers Press; quoted more liberally from a few other authors; somewhat rewritten the introduction; and added what I hope are helpful comments and explanations under some of the entries.

INTRODUCTION

'So in the café in that vile city of Reading, I said I'd marry him.'
— Dora Carrington to Lytton Strachey, 14 May 1921

Carrington, painter and 'Bloomsberry', was not the first visitor to assume that Reading was a city, nor the last to call it vile; but her epithet is more an indication of emotional turmoil than a considered opinion of the town. The quotations that follow – almost all by outsiders – by no means constitute a wholly favourable press. To begin with the good news: some writers have found Reading variously a live town; a vigorous town; handsomely built; interesting, prosperous and pleasant; a most genial centre. Moving down the scale, the praise becomes decidedly faint with phrases like useful, very useful; most unpretentious; Britain's average town;

not exciting; commonplace in the extreme; not wholly Golgotha; awful, dull, flat anonymity. When it comes to outright damnation, the words are unminced: frankly depressing; frankly ugly; utter scrappiness; calculated squalor; a stupendous octopus; administratively half-baked, artistically null, and architecturally hideous. That last trio is from Alan Wykes, who lived nearby and went on to write a 'biography' of Reading: the blurb on its dust-jacket tells of his affection for the place.

I have arranged the pieces chronologically, which normally means in order of first publication; but in the case of letters, diaries and travelogues I have used the date of writing, where known. The reader will note some peaks and troughs on the Readingometer, with a lot of choppy water in between. Early visitors (who include some household names) were just passing, and concerned mainly with the customer service rating of the inns they stopped at. William Mavor, whose real interest was pigs and peas, tells us what strangers will find irresistibly attractive about the town; but hard on his heels comes 'The Stranger' himself, the anonymous and wonderfully dyspeptic Mr Man, blundering like Mr Magoo into every possible kind of obstruction on the footways. He should be made a posthumous president of the Pedestrians' Association.

Mid-nineteenth-century writers tended to see Progress and Prosperity, but in the great late-Victorian and Edwardian age of pleasure-boating the majority of tourists came to Reading by default, because it happened to have been built near the Thames. Accounts of their voyages, and guide-books to help them through, proliferated (and copied each other: note the multiple references to George Palmer, the baggy-trousered philanthropist): the more readable ones have furnished the watery backbone of this collection. It cannot be denied that if you had sculled down through honeyed Cotswold villages, or skiffed under the mellow, yellow walls of Oxford, or steamed past crisp white stucco riverside mansions in the Goring Gap, your first sight of Reading's riparian factories was a grotty shock, and many visitors never stepped ashore to see what delights might have lain behind the grimy bricks. The long series of have-a-go-at-Reading pieces was started wittily, and perhaps not altogether wittingly, by none other than Jerome K Jerome. But only two years after him came the Pennells, who – with artists' eyes – waded in to the town's defence. One author I had hoped to quote was Thomas Hardy: I re-read *Jude the Obscure*, hoping to find a nice gloomy description of 'Aldbrickham', but was disappointed.

Unsurprisingly, Johns Betjeman and Piper in the thirties and forties strove to make people look about them more carefully and to appreciate unfashionable things like terracotta shopfronts. Arthur Mee's eulogy reads laughably now: to him even Slough takes on a tint of rose. Of the post-war pen-picturers, Eric de Maré disappointingly failed to see anything photogenic in the industrial and waterway landscapes. A fresh bottle of vitriol was broached by Alan Wykes; but as the last heavy industries closed, and Reading was moved bodily from the valley of the Alder to that of the Silicon, the focus

of criticism shifted to a perceived dullness, averageness, and anonymity. Anthony Burton took this line: he is in the tradition of Ian Nairn and Ray Gosling, careful wordsmiths who try hard to pin down the character of a town, perhaps just because they see so many places becoming so mistakable. In the late 20th and early 21st centuries there is a trend towards cynical, throw-away comments; shall we ever return to a more thoughtful era?

A few specific topics deserve attention. First, the Three Bs Bar under the Town Hall is an excellent *rathskeller,* but the euphonious 'Beer, Biscuits and Bulbs', supposedly the foundation of Reading's prosperity, is a recent coinage. The original tag, from a piece of verse quoted below by Ryan (1938), was 'Biscuits, Seeds and Sauce', the last being Cocks's. The presence of one or more breweries in a town this size was not noteworthy until the 1960s, and Reading's industries had for long been more diverse, notably including printing and ironworks; also boxes (metal, for the biscuits) and bricks – the fourth and fifth Bs. Many of the writers quoted below noticed Reading's bricks, but where they saw bricks they only saw red: virtually no-one mentions the polychrome and inventive patterning that makes Victorian Reading such a pleasure to walk around. They also go on about uniformity of design, when in fact many streets were built in little campaigns of two, four or six houses at a time, conforming to a common building line and overall shape but showing pleasing variations.

A word about Caversham, annexed by Reading in 1911. Salters' Guide to the Thames labelled it 'a well-to-do suburb – Reading's Richmond', but Derry (1899) lumbered it with all of Reading's industry, and Robertson (1937) must surely have had some personal grudge against it.

Real tourists do visit Reading. Back in the days when we could afford a Tourist Information Centre, their Visitors' Book revealed that they came for all sorts of reasons: embroidery, postcards, tanners, Being Earnest; some hailed from Reading (USA), others were from Reading (UK) but had been called away for 50 years. And the current residents? A stand-up comic at the Hexagon once asked his audience what happened here, and the shouted answers were 'football', 'shopping' and 'bondage'.

I wonder whether any other town of Reading's size has provoked so many and such various comments. I cannot claim to have invented a genre; I know of two similar compilations, both of which predate mine: Eric Stokes's *The Things they say about Basingstoke* (2nd edition, 1997) and *Bath in Quotes* by Paul Cresswell (1985). Stephen Bunker's account of 19th century Luton, *Strawopolis* (1999) devotes several pages to opinions of the town, and finds, as I did in Reading, widely discrepant views expressed by different writers within a year or two.

If this little anthology seems to give an overall thumbs-down to Reading, I take some of the blame: it does not pretend to be balanced, and pannings always make better reading than rave reviews. In giving these extracts a fresh airing I do not mean to encourage the habit of denigrating one's home town; I hope rather that readers will look anew at their surroundings, and appreciate what is good about Reading – or at least what still distinguishes it from Elsewhere.

Many thanks to Reading Central Library, and especially the Local Studies staff, for help and hospitality; to all who have kindly drawn my attention to source material; to Reg Martin for letting me raid his collection of waterways literature; to John Froy and Barbara Morris of Two Rivers for their painstaking proofreading and constructive comments; and the following authors, publishers for permission to quote from copyright material:

Tom Fort; Norman Scarfe (*Innocent Espionage*); Merlin Holland (*Selected Letters of Oscar Wilde*: © Estate of Oscar Wilde 1962); A. & C. Black (Publishers) Ltd. (*Buckingham and Berkshire* and *The Thames*); The Trustees of Mrs H. M. Davies (*Poet's Pilgrimage*); Alexander Maclehose & Co. (*On Foot in Berkshire*); Laurence Pollinger Ltd. and the estate of Robert Gibbings (*Sweet Thames Run Softly*); John Murray (Publishers) Ltd. (*Murray's Berkshire Architectural Guide*); Orion Publishing Group (*Thirteen Rivers to the Thames*); Peter Fraser and Dunlop Group Ltd. (*An Eye on the Thames*); Robert Hale Ltd. (*Portrait of the Thames*); Little, Brown & Co. (UK) (*Thames Passport*); David Higham Associates (*Back Door Britain*); Roger Jones (*Green Road to Land's End*); Constable & Co. (*A Guide to the Thames path*). Every effort has been made to contact copyright holders; I apologise to anyone who has been inadvertently omitted.

ANTHOLOGY

Henry I built this monastery between the rivers Kennet and Thames, in a spot calculated for the reception of almost all who might have occasion to travel to the most populous cities of England, where he placed monks of the Cluniac order, who are at this day a noble pattern of holiness, and an example of unwearied and delightful hospitality.

— **WILLIAM OF MALMESBURY:** *Gesta Regum Anglorum*, c1126; translation by J. B. Hurry in *Reading Abbey* (1901)

Reading's written history starts in 870, but we have to wait 250 years for the first recorded opinion. It makes a good start for the fledgling Abbey (and for this anthology). The DNB calls William 'England's greatest national and local historian since Bede, and the most learned European of his day'.

There is a park cumming into Reading toun belonging to the late monasterie there. There is no manner of token that ever the toun of Reading was waullid; yet it is a very auncient toun, and at this tyme the best toun of al Barkshire. There was a castelle in the Saxons tyme ... I could not perceive or clerely lerne wher it stood. But by al likelihood at the west-ende of the Castelle-Streat: and, as sum thinke, about the place of execution ... peradventure it stoode wher thabbay was. [Reading is] a pleasant abode, furnished with good yeomanry, and placed midst fruitful pasture.

—**JOHN LELAND:** *The Itinerary*, 1539

470 years have passed, and still no-one has 'perceived or clearly learnt' where Reading's castle stood.

From hence he little Chausey seeth, and hasteneth for to see
Fair Redinge towne, a place of name, where cloths ywoven bee.
— JOHN LELAND: *Cantio Cygnea*, 1545 (from the Latin: quoted in John Man's
History, 1816)

This little town for the neatnesse of its streets and the finenesse of its
buildings, for its riches and the reputation it hath gotten for making of
cloath, goes beyond all the other towns of this county.
— WILLIAM CAMDEN: *Britannia*, 1586

And as this famous towne, for pleasant situation and rich commodities,
for prudent government and civill state, but especially for the plentiful
means of knowledge and grace, is as a light set up in a candlestick, or as a
tower on the top of an hill, and a beacon to the whole countrie ...
— THOMAS TAYLOR, 1621
    Taylor, a Puritan divine, was sometimes known as 'a brazen wall against
    popery'.

And from thence I passt through ye Countryes till I came to Readinge &
there was a few yt [that] had beene convinced: & on ye first day In Geo:
Lambells orcharde almost all ye whole tounde came together & there
came two of judges ffells daughters to mee: & Geo: Bishoppe with his
sworde by his syde: & a glorious meetinge it was & a great convincement
of people there was yt day: & people was mightily satisfyed. And many
baptists & ranters came privately after meetinge reasoninge & disputinge
butt ye Lords power came over ym [them] all: & ye ranters pleaded yt
God made ye Divell but I denied it ...
— GEORGE FOX: *Journal*, 1655
    Fox founded the Society of Friends, alias the Quakers. Later in this journey he
    was imprisoned at Launceston.

16 June: ... and in the evening betimes came to Reding, and there heard
my wife read more of Mustapha. Then to supper, and then I to walk about
the town, which is a very great one, I think bigger than Salisbury: a river
runs through it in seven branches, and unite in one, in one part of the
town, and runs into the Thames ...

17 June: Rose, and paying the reckoning, 12*s* 6*d*; servants and poor,
2*s* 6*d*; music, the worst we have heard, coming to our chamber-door, but

calling us by wrong names, we gave him nothing.
— SAMUEL PEPYS: *Diary*, 1668

Redding ... which is a pretty large place, severall Churches, in one lyes buried one of my sisters that dyed at my Grandmothers there of the small pox, her monument of white marble stands up in the Chancell.

Reading is the shire town its pretty large, accomodated for travellers, being a great Road to Glocester and the West Country but it is very dear.
— CELIA FIENNES: *Journal*, c1691 and c1701

Fiennes was one of the first women to take up serious tourism, supposedly to improve her health; she visited every English county, often staying with her extensive family connections. Historians are grateful to her for taking an interest in new houses, mines, industry and spas. Her punctuation and spelling never improved: she rendered 'Basingstoke' in three ways within five lines. Nor was her observation too keen: the Uffington white horse she saw as 'the perfect shape off a horse'. The sister was Ann, who died in infancy in 1675; the monument, in St Giles's church, curiously calls her 'Mrs'.

This is truly a town of meeting: of the waters of rivers, and of these friends in a place kept tidy for the spirit of Jesus Christ.
— WILLIAM PENN, C1705

A plaque in the Reading International Solidarity Centre on London Street records that 'William Penn (founder of Pennsylvania) worshipped here 1711–1715'. The great Quaker died at Ruscombe in 1718.

The town of Reading is very pleasantly situated, and it is large, nothing near so famous now for cloathing as it was formerly. The houses are very mean, and the streetes, though pretty large, unpaved. The occasion of the houses being so mean is this. The greatest part of them belong to one Blagrave, and his interest in them being only for lives, there is no likelihood of their being rebuilt as yet.

— THOMAS HEARNE: *Journey to Reading and Silchester*, 1714 (published in *Letters to Eminent Persons*, 1813)

Hearne, born at White Waltham, became an antiquary and a librarian at the Bodleian, and edited the works of Leland and Camden. He didn't believe that William Stukeley had discovered an amphitheatre at Silchester. A legal case about the Blagrave 'leases for lives' was rumbling on in 1829.

A very large and wealthy town, handsomely built, the inhabitants rich and driving a very great trade.

— DANIEL DEFOE: *Tour through the Whole Island of Great Britain*, 1724

At this place I observed a vast expense but laid out without either taste or judgment. The house consists of various parts irregularly put together as his Lordship's fancy or occasion required it.

— SIR JOHN CLERK on Caversham Park, 1727

The house, long since rebuilt, was then very new; Earl (William) Cadogan, whose name lives on in a Caversham pub, had it put up in 1723.

... Dr Anthony Addington was Pitt's family doctor and a former keeper of a private madhouse at Reading – a town which, he claimed, without giving his reasons for an assertion that cannot have endeared him to its inhabitants, contained an unusually high proportion of lunatics.

If we may believe Dr Addington in his examination before the House of Commons, the people of Reading were very much inclined to be cracked brains.

— c1750: quoted by Christopher Hibbert in *George IV, Prince of Wales*, 1972; seconded by John Man in his unpublished *Anecdotes*, c1805

Addington's son Henry became Viscount Sidmouth.

This town, in my opinion, may be styl'd a pretty one, but residing there three years near may perhaps have made me partial. 'Tis finely situated on the rivers Thames and Kennet. There are several good streets, and the market-place is neat and spacious. ... The adjoining Faubourg, which commands one of the finest views I ever saw, contains the venerable ruins of an ancient abbey, founded by Henry I, who was there buried, but his bones (as Rapin says), were thrown out to make a stable, and the monastery is now a dwelling-house. ... Reading has three handsome churches built in the quincunx fashion; and within a furlong of the town, to the south-west, within a hundred yards of the Kennet, on a rise called Cat's grove hill, is a stratum of oysters, five or six inches through the hill, many large and entire, others mould'ring and decayed, supposed to have been there buried at the Deluge.

— MRS LYBBE POWIS: *Diaries*, 1759–60

Mrs Powis lived at Hardwick House, between Caversham and Whitchurch.

'Quincunx fashion' refers to the flint and stone chequerwork, best seen on St Mary's tower, which the eye reads in groups of five.

I preached at Reading. Several soldiers were there and many more the next night, when I set before them 'the terrors of the Lord' and I scarce ever saw so much impression on this dull, senseless people.

In the evening I preached at Reading. How many years were we beating the air at this town? Stretching out our hands to a people stupid as oxen! But it is not so at present. That generation is passed away, and their children are of a more excellent spirit.

— JOHN WESLEY: *Journals*, 1755 and 1777

Wesley could be intemperate, and readily made enemies. In 1755 he was having marital difficulties.

When the Earth was first divided,
Reading was a favourite spot,
'Twas there, decency resided,
Rul'd the rich, and blessed the Cot.
Industry, owned all the traders,
Far and near their fame resound;
Smiling wealth bless'd all their labours,
All with Independence crown'd.

— JOHN MAN: *Anecdotes* (unpublished MS, c1785)

Man wrote Reading's second history (1816) and also the much more entertaining 'The Stranger in Reading' – see entry at 1810 below.

This town abounds in inns and I daresay that the worst would be found excellent in other parts of the country. We weren't staying in the best, but it was one of the best we have ever stayed in. The house is large and clean, the stables likewise: a garden of 2½ acres, full of canals for keeping fish alive in two garden-rooms used for taking tea in summer; a small kitchen-garden, hot-houses and a waterfall. I haven't mentioned that we were served by two men with powdered hair.

— FRANÇOIS DE LA ROCHEFOUCAULD: *Travel Journal*, 1785 (published as *Innocent Espionage*, translated by Norman Scarfe, 1995)
  On an extensive tour of England, Rochefoucauld and his brother took an intelligent interest in everything they saw, but especially the early manifestations of the industrial revolution.

I rode over Sonning Bridge to Caversham: my observation, by the way, was on the many human pairs I met: some lovers, some past their love; and I could with a certainty pronounce how near matrimony was, or how long committed, by their civility or rudeness; some scarcely approaching; others squeezing hands; and of those married a twelvemonth, the poor woman carrying the child, the husband scorning to give assistance. Mr Loveday's family were in tolerable plight and, as usual, happy to see me. My visit was to announce our intention of breakfasting with them the next morning; so after parading the garden with his daughters, and sitting some time with Mr Loveday over his fruit, we took our leave and were at the Black Bear, Reading, before our ladies arrived. Supper order'd, and quickly served, with a bowl (again) of sour and weak punch; we sat up till eleven o'clock, and were cheerful; but when I went to bed, I fancied the sheets damp and so to my sides there were only blankets.

— JOHN BYNG (5th Viscount Torrington): *Of a Tour into South Wales*, 1787
  The Lovedays lived at The Old Rectory, Caversham; its garden survives as Caversham Court.

We were very near meeting with an Accident in Reading, passing a Waggon, but thank God we got by safe and well. It was owing to the Coachman. As we went out of Reading we met a Regiment of Soldiers, some Militia going into Reading. At Reading there were two young Gentlemen by name Joliffe that got up on the top of the Coach, being going home from School for the Vacation. I remembered their Father at Winchester School.

— JAMES WOODFORDE: *The Diary of a Country Parson,* 1793

Where silver Kennet, like a wedded dame,
Loses in Thames' embrace, her native name,
Pleas'd Thames beholds bright READING rear the head,
'Mid characters of age still faintly read,
Defenceless bulwarks, now a peaceful walk,
Huge, mouldring walls, where plaintive echoes talk,
Retreats for holy contemplation made,
With trim-built houses, and with gardens green,
Which o'er the ruins shine, a motley scene,
As whiten'd spires on antique turrets show,
Or on some aged oak, the mistletoe.

Such Reading was, but hence shall it be,
Illustrious Oxford, next in fame to thee;
And Thames and Isis shall contend no more,
Now one in honour, as in streams before,
For, here too Science, at her sons' request,
Consents to sojourn, an eternal guest,
Auspicious aerea! Which shall late descend.
Embalm'd, in record, as fair learning's friend,
And, gathering favour, as confirmed in worth,
Reflect in manhood splendour on its birth.

— JOHN BERKELEY MONCK: *Verses on the opening of the Reading Literary Institution,* 1808

Monck was a politician. The Institution did not quite rival Oxford University.

Distant 39 miles from London, and delightfully situated on a general ascent from the Thames, and washed by the Kennet, which flows nearly through the centre in several streams, and falls into the prince of British rivers, about a furlong below the town. The houses are chiefly built of brick, well built, and commodious; and the streets are spaciously and handsomely paved. An air of gentility is thrown over the place; and there is an elegant sociability in the manners of its inhabitants, which is irresistibly attractive to strangers. Hence villas are constantly rising in its vicinity; nor is this to be wondered at, as there is not a country town in the kingdom that unites so many charms and advantages to persons of independent fortune, and cultivated minds.

Reading contains three parishes, 1787 houses, and a population of 9742 souls, which is constantly increasing. It is governed by a mayor, aldermen, &c, and returns two members to parliament, who are chosen by the inhabitants paying scot and lot, amounting to about 600. The spring assizes are held here; the Epiphany, and sometimes the Michaelmas seasons. The grammar school is in high reputation, under the direction of Dr Valpy, and is an ornament and advantage to the town; which in every respect, is the first in Berkshire, though it divides the honour of the county with Abingdon.

— **WILLIAM FORDYCE MAVOR:** *General View of the Agriculture of Berkshire,* 1809

I could not help remarking a custom, which, however *odd* it may appear to strangers, is almost universally adopted here: I mean, that of having a *pretty little* dunghill before each house, composed of road dirt, ashes, straw, dung, turnip parings, cabbage leaves, &c, &c. but these last are not so plentiful as might be *wished,* owing to some all-devouring hogs, who are continually plundering these precious compounds of the greater part of *their beauty.*

… Among the nuisances, that embarrass the passages of this populous town, may be reckoned *umbrellas*; these are now used by every class, from the peer,

the parson, or the magistrate down to the porter or the pot-girl. For this reason, I seldom go out on a wet day, there being then no passing these formidable barriers without being *blessed* with a pailfull of water down your back, or having one of *your eyes* thrust out with the brass ends of the ribs, extending for this express purpose, two inches beyond the silk covering.

... There is one remark a *stranger* cannot fail to make in this place; and that is, the number of bald-headed people he is in the daily habit of seeing: at first, I thought this phenomenon might be owing to their well-water, which is strongly impregnated with the sulphate of lime ...

— JOHN MAN: *The Stranger in Reading*, 1810 (new edition from Two Rivers Press, 2005)
Man published this book anonymously as a series of letters, purportedly from a Londoner who spent a year in Reading. In fact the author, a retired schoolmaster, had lived in the town for 40 years and knew it intimately.

Reading was built by Henry I, who was buried here, as was likewise his Queen, and his daughter Maud. On a hill near Reading is a remarkable Bed of Oyster Shells, of which an account is given in the Philosophical Transactions. The chief trade of Reading is in Malt.
— *Paterson's Roads*, 1811

I always said, and you were always in a passion when I did say it, that the Reading coach people, the Reading post people, and Reading altogether, was the most careless, blundering, unpunctual town ever heard of.

... I have not, however, any notion that we shall migrate far from this neighbourhood; and, to tell you the truth, am desperately afraid of the famous and patriotic borough of Reading, which papa likes, for its newspaper and its justice-rooms and its elections; and which I dislike for various negative reasons.

A sad Jacobinical town, illustrious and quarrelsome borough.

A town of negations that Reading is – no tree – no flowers – no green fields – no wit – no literature – no elegance! Neither the society of London nor the freedom of the country. We never say a word about it, for or against – never mention the illustrious dull town; but I expect that some fine morning papa will come back and have taken a house there.

… Not that I have any quarrel with that illustrious town, which, as Grey said of Cambridge, 'would be well enough if it were not for the people'; but those people – their gossiping – their mistiness – the dense fogs that hang about them! Oh! You can imagine nothing so bad. They are as rusty as old iron and as jagged as flint stones.

— **MARY RUSSELL MITFORD**: letters, 1813, 1819 and 1820

Miss Mitford's fame rests on her sketches of rural life in Three Mile Cross (*Our Village*) and urban life in Reading (*Belford Regis*). In the latter book (see 1835 entry below) she is polite about the town, but her private views are among the first to express general disapproval.

The local situation of Reading is such, as to claim the notice of the first Metropolis in the known world, London; and being so pleasantly situated on the high road from the second Metropolis in this Kingdom, Bristol, and the most elegant and fashionable City of Europe, Bath, it cannot fail to attract and become a retreat to the independent part of society. … Reading appears to be a nursery to Commerce, the youth being destined to branch out under her banners into every part of the World, therefore the connection will always be respectable and numerous to inhabit a description of Houses of this superior order.

— **THOMAS JESSE** in the *Reading Mercury*, 1817

This was salesman's talk, from a property developer who wanted to build a Grand Square off the Bath Road, somewhere near the present Jesse Terrace.

I am delighted with the people that I have seen at Reading.

— **WILLIAM COBBETT**: *Rural Rides*, 1822

Writer, agriculturalist and politician, Cobbett was no lover of towns; Reading escaped lightly.

Where from flower-bordered meadows flows the stream
Of ancient Kennet; till at length it joins
The fuller waters of old Father Thames,
Stands red-faced Reading, blushing in the sun.
A town so ancient, none can trace its birth,
Nor tell the story of its earliest days.
Old is its ruined Abbey; older far
The town in which good Henry founded it.

— Quoted by J. J. Cooper in *Some Worthies of Reading*, 1923 from an earlier
publication called *Tales of Old Reading*. This I have not been able to track
down.

Cheerfulness is, perhaps, the word that best describes the impression conveyed by the more frequented streets of Belford. It is not a manufacturing town, and its trade is solely that dependent on its own population, and the demands of a thickly inhabited neighbourhood; so that, except in the very centre of that trade, the streets where the principal shops are congregated, or on certain public occasions, such as elections, fairs, and markets, the stir hardly amounts to bustle. Neither is it a professed place of gaiety, like Cheltenham or Brighton; where London people go to find or make a smaller London out of town. It is neither more nor less than an honest English borough, fifty good miles from 'the deep, deep sea,' and happily free from the slightest suspicion of any spa, chalybeate or saline. We have, it is true, 'the Kennet swift, for silver eels renowned,' passing through the walls, and the mighty Thames for a near neighbour – water in plenty, but luckily all fresh! ... Clean, airy, orderly, and affluent; well paved, well lighted, well watched; abounding in wide and spacious streets, filled with excellent shops and handsome houses; – such is the outward appearance, the bodily form, of our market-town. For the vital spirit, the life-blood that glows and circulates through the dead mass of mortar and masonry – in other words, for the inhabitants – I must refer my courteous reader to the following pages.

— MARY RUSSELL MITFORD: *Belford Regis*, 1835

Presumably Miss Mitford changed the name of the town (and the dedications

of its parish churches) in case some of the inhabitants recognised themselves; but she kept the river names, and everyone knew where she lived. A chalybeate well had in fact been discovered at Surley Row in 1803, but Emmer Green never became a full-blown spa.

… this sober town which assumes all the gravity and dignity which ought assuredly to belong to so ancient and venerable a borough. It appears as staid as the massy ruins and antique buildings of which it is composed; as unchangeable as their time-enduring walls, and as immovable as their foundations. There is a tone of quiet sobriety and stability; with a staunch, unbending firmness, in the aspect of this old-fashioned capital of this royal and beautiful county, seldom to be found in the present state of cities and towns. Like the slow-moving and deeply-freighted ship, sailing majestically along, untossed by the waves, so has this town glided deliberately down, almost unchanged, through ages of time.

— WILLIAM FLETCHER: *Reading Past and Present*, 1839

The date is significant: a year later the railway would start Reading's headlong rush into the future.

A town whose dignity may appear to be irretrievably lost in squalor, but which can be captured by the united efforts of its citizens.

— EDWARD OLIVER, c1839

Oliver, a retired bank clerk, was a 'champion' of the new Royal Berks Hospital.

Got on the Railway at Reading and travelled by that mode the last 38 miles. The carriage was the most superb of any railway carriage I ever saw, a regular drawing room with large plate glass windows, and two tables surrounded by velvet sofas. The motion, however, the worst I know on any rails.

— BARCLAY FOX: *Journal*, 13 May 1840

Fox was sampling the GWR in its second month, and appreciating the spacious accommodation provided by the broad gauge. For such an early rail passenger he had more experience than most: this was his fourth journey.

The rowing down from Oxford to Reading, on the Thames, is more charming than I can describe in words. I rowed down last June, through miles upon miles of water-lilies, lying on the water close together, like a fairy pavement. But once arrived in Reading the enchantment is gone. A soporific atmosphere takes command, brought about by enervation, which in turn is ordered by the tranquillity of the river as it drains away with it the energies of the people. It is not unlike a blood-letting, and, like that device, probably drains away with it many of the common fluxes of illness, for I never saw fewer people ill or in any way upset.

— CHARLES DICKENS: letter to Angela Burdett-Coutts, c1843

Dickens gave readings in Reading and was president of the Literary and Mechanics' Institution; but he declined an invitation to represent it in Parliament.

On rising ground, at the entrance to Reading, and close to the venerable abbey, this new prison is from every side the most conspicuous building, and architecturally, by far the greatest ornament in the town.

— *The Illustrated London News*, 1844

The 'ornament' is still there; it was the work of the young George Gilbert Scott in a brief partnership with William Bonython Moffat.

Reading is nothing but an extended cesspool.

— DR THOMAS SOUTHWOOD SMITH, social reformer, in a report for the Royal Commission into the Health of Towns, 1846

The town of Reading has been often described, its history often written. Whoever has read 'Belford Regis' – and who has not? – knows something

of the sunny side of its present condition; and the readers of this series of volumes have had a lively picture set before them of its state at one period of its older existence. ... It is a large irregularly arranged place (though I believe the historians of the town have found out some definite shape for it, but whether triangle or hexangle, I forget) ... It has three old churches, which have been all miserably defaced, and look miserable; one or two new ones, which look very smart; and one or two others, which look very shabby. It has also the usual number of dissenting chapels, which present the usual varieties of deformity. Finally there are the workhouse and the county gaol. So that it has altogether a very comfortable, respectable, social, substantial, every-day English look.

— JAMES THORNE: *Rambles by Rivers*, 1847

> The approximate triangle's points were the Town Hall, Greyfriars and Whitley Pump. In the 1970s the Council chose a hexagonal logo and built a hexagonal Civic Centre and entertainment venue – both now life-expired. As to the old churches, in 1847 St Laurence still had the 1619 'piazza' stuck onto its south aisle, St Giles had been Georgianized, and Greyfriars was derelict.

Reading is a credit to the beautiful river that sweeps through its valley; neat, active, bustling – a sort of miniature city, with a sprinkling of pretty villas in pleasant suburbs.

— MR & MRS S.C. HALL: *The Book of the Thames*, 1859

The town is associated in a somewhat grotesque manner with two eminent names – those of John Bunyan, and S.T. Coleridge; the former being accustomed, in those days when nonconformist preaching was anything but safe, 'to go through the town dressed like a carter, and with a long whip in his hand, to avoid detection;' and the latter having been found on one occasion reading 'Horace' in a tap-room, at the time when he had enlisted himself as a soldier in the 15th Dragoons. On enquiring the name of this learned 'private,' it was found to be Silas Tomkins Cumberbatch.

— ANON: *The Thames from Oxford to the Sea*, 1859

It takes three centuries to carry anything out in Reading: one to think about it, one to talk about it, and another to carry it out.

— JOHN OKEY TAYLOR, mayor-elect, 1862

> This gibe is a borrowing from John Man's *The Stranger in Reading* – see 1810 above.

Reading is a vigorous town, distinguished for an energetic individuality during a consecutive history a thousand years long. It bears its antiquity with great elasticity, and in the matter of progress will never do discredit to its dozen namesakes in America. It is situated on a bright, busy little river called the Kennet, a mile or two above its junction with the Thames. It now numbers about 20,000 inhabitants, and may see that number doubled, and even trebled, before it ceases to grow. It has been

the mother of men who have made their mark on history; some of them, unfortunately, a rather black mark. ... The Reading of today is, as I have already said, a live town, full of healthful activities. It is distinguished for four establishments which have given it an honourable status and reputation at home and abroad. The three first have to do with the staff of life, and they do a great work in that field of enterprise. The fourth is a very extensive institution for repairing the breaches of society, by punishing criminals and turning them out safer men and women. Although so unlike the other three, this last has much connexion with them. Barrett and Exall's manufactory of agricultural implements produces an immense amount of diversified machinery for cultivating the soil, and growing all kinds of grain and roots for man and beast. Huntley and Palmer's biscuit manufactory can work up into its world of cakes all the wheat that their neighbours' ploughs, drills and threshing-machines can produce when well-manned on the best soil. Sutton and Sons, the great seedsmen, can furnish seeds of every earthly description enough for a small continent. And the Reading gaol can house and discipline all the idle and vicious people of a county who are not content to earn and eat their bread in the sweat of an honest brow, but go poaching upon the peace of society with their evil passions and habits.

— ELIHU BURRITT: *A Walk from London to Land's End and Back*, 1864

The book continues with a seven-page description of the biscuit factory. Burritt, born in Connecticut, was at various times a blacksmith, multilinguist, U.S. Commercial Consul in Birmingham, traveller, lecturer and peace campaigner. Miss Mitford (see entries at 1813 and 1835 above) relates in a letter that she heard him speak on 'Peace and Progress' in Reading in 1832, though most sources claim that he didn't visit the UK until 1846. He was probably the first person to set out to walk to both Land's End and John O'Groats, though he did cheat a little.

23

I must explain that I had no personal dislike to the biscuit-making chimneys – on the contrary, I thought their perpendicular lines were rather pleasant in the distant valley; but I do own to a feeling of irritation when every visitor looking at the view found it necessary to tell me that these were Huntley and Palmers' chimneys!

— GERTRUDE JEKYLL, quoted in George Leslie's *Our River*, published 1881
　Miss Jekyll, the great gardener, lived at Wargrave Manor from 1868 to 1877.

Not far, another [town] lies, whose life just gives
The faintest image of those northern hives,
Where man, it seemeth, but to labour lives,
Where one toils for wealth, for food another strives.

— JOHN STAPLETON: *The Thames*, 1878
　Perhaps the image wasn't so faint: Reading was well industrialized by this
　date.

Reading folks do not seem much addicted to aquatics, and the boats let out for hire about here are just the sort to suit what Mr Calderon used to call 'drowning parties'. No-one judging from the ignominious junction of the Kennet with the Thames would imagine what a pretty, cheerful stream it is nearer to its source.

— GEORGE D. LESLIE: *Our River*, 1881

Reading itself is a very interesting town. It is built of red brick, and the Salvation Army does a great business there. You can enjoy yourself at Reading very much, indeed. The dentist's name is Harvey. Huntley and Palmer's biscuit factory is at Reading. All these facts are well worthy of notice. There is a great philanthropist at Reading whom everybody knows. He is about as kind a man as ever lived, only he hasn't reduced charity to an exact science.

— ARTHUR T. PASK: *From Lock to Lock, a Playful Guide to the Thames*, 1882
　The Philanthropist was presumably George Palmer.

The streets, which are numerous, are many of them well-built imposing thoroughfares, but it is singular, considering the few vicissitudes which have occurred, and how seldom the Town has been assailed by important disturbing causes, so little should remain that is illustrative of the architectural peculiarities of past ages. A few ancient domestic memorials certainly may be observed in nearly every street, but they are nothing more than mere gabled frontages, entirely destitute of either character or magnitude. ... It will be seen that Orthodoxy and Heterodoxy are fully provided for in the town of Reading, but the state of the streets on Sunday evenings proclaim that much, as yet, has to be done to entice the people within the walls of the various edifices.

— GEORGE HILLIER: *The Stranger's Guide to the Town of Reading*, 1882
  Hillier's Stranger, which went through several editions, is much less fun
  (and less strange) than Man's (see 1810 above).

Reading folks are proverbially slow in adopting new ideas, and in the winter-time our working classes have no choice between saintliness and sin; no reading-rooms, no oratories, no recreation of any sort – and it behoves us to make early provision for their rational entertainment at a time when they really stand in need of it.

— *The Berkshire Bell*, 1884
  The *Bell* was a high-minded but short-lived local periodical.

We came to Reading prepared for anything but charm in that town of biscuits, and we were not inclined to alter our ready-made opinion upon sight of it. We passed through 'double-quick', leaving the last of the town as late as 8.30. He who runs may read, perhaps, if the type be sufficiently large; but I don't think he would find it possible to write: we did not, and so this book must go forth lacking a description of Reading.

— CHARLES G. HARPER: *From Paddington to Penzance*, 1884 (published 1893)
  Harper arrived in a rowing-boat and departed by train.

We came in sight of Reading about eleven. The river is dirty and dismal here. One does not linger in the neighbourhood of Reading. The town itself is a famous old place, dating from the dim days of Ethelred, when the Danes anchored their warships in the Kennet, and started from Reading to ravage all the lands of Wessex; and here Ethelred and his brother Alfred fought and defeated them, Ethelred doing the praying and Alfred the fighting.

In later years, Reading seems to have been regarded as a handy place to run down to, when matters were becoming unpleasant in London. Parliament generally rushed off to Reading whenever there was a plague on at Westminster and, in 1625, the Law followed suit, and all the courts were held at Reading. It must have been worthwhile having a mere ordinary plague now and then in London to get rid of both the lawyers and the Parliament.

Even Reading, though it does its best to spoil and sully and make hideous as much of the river as it can reach, is good-natured enough to keep its ugly face a good deal out of sight.

— JEROME K. JEROME: *Three Men in a Boat*, 1889

The trains on the Great Western railway average about an hour from Paddington; from Waterloo about an hour and three-quarters; and from Charing Cross three hours or more. Population, about 48,000. Death rate, 18 per 1000. Soil, chalk and gravel. There is a good and constant supply of water from the water-works, and a system of mains drainage with an irrigation farm about two miles from the borough. Reading can lay claim to great antiquity, and is the most important and flourishing town in the county of Berkshire. It is a parliamentary and municipal borough, represented by Mr T. C Murdoch, a conservative. It is a well-built town with fine broad streets and many excellent shops, and is evidently well cared for, although it is understood that the various improvements which have been carried out by the corporation, and the general cost of local government, have raised the burdens on the ratepayers to an inconvenient if not excessive amount.

— CHARLES DICKENS (JUNIOR): *Dickens's Dictionary of the Thames, an Unconventional Handbook*, 1890

Paddington is now 25 minutes away; Waterloo a tedious 82 (this line was faster in 1945); the Charing Cross route – via Guildford, Redhill and Croydon – was prettier, but never a sensible option, and would today come in at just under two hours. The 1893 edition of the Dictionary was reprinted in 1972 by Taurus Press.

From here [Mapledurham] to Caversham is the stupid stretch of which guide and other books give fair warning. But at the hour of sunset the ugliest country is glorified, and nowhere is the river really ugly. ... The town of Reading ... seldom has a good word said for it by those who write from the river point of view. And yet the stream of the Thames makes glad the city with its railways and big brick factories and tall chimneys, and it becomes, in its own way, picturesque, though not as characteristic of the upper Thames, as the little villages and the old deserted towns. It is not, however, the ideal place for a house-boat, and for this reason, I suppose, we found two or three within hearing of the ever-passing trains and within sight of the chimneys and the smoke. From them, canoes were carrying young men and their luggage to the convenient station; in the small boats at their bows young ladies were lounging; in the stern white-capped maids were busy with brooms and buckets.

— JOSEPH AND ELIZABETH PENNELL: *The Stream of Pleasure*, 1891

The Pennells were a Philadelphian artist (he) and writer (she) who travelled widely in Europe, often by unconventional means: apart from several boat trips they walked, cycled, tandemmed, tricycled and even motor-tricycled.

Huntley and Palmers' Great Biscuit Manufactory

O! who has not heard of old Reading's famed town,
So widely made known by the industry there,
Whose goods are sent forth both east, west, south and north,
And with which for quality none can compare.

'Tis built on the banks of old Kennet's fair stream,
And 'tween it the river doth silently flow,
Neat bridges stretch o'er, thus connecting each shore,
Their useful long arms o'er the water they throw.

And on either side spacious buildings appear,
Which cover vast acres of wide stretching space;
With red brick and stone, due proportion is shown,
And all well arranged in their own proper place.

Tall shafts tow'ring upwards and piercing the sky
Like mainmasts that stretch from the deck down below,
Whence borne far away where with clouds it can play,
The smoke in huge columns doth heavenwards go.

And O! what machinery working within,
In seeming confusion that puzzles the mind
How it rattles and hums, its rollers and drums
And slow trav'lling ovens that evermore wind.

… No firm equal to it old England can boast,
Nor indeed can the world its rival e'er show;
Where biscuits and cakes of all sizes and makes
Impregnate the air with the odours they throw.

… O! gigantic firm! 'tis the stay of the town,
Without it we could not long very well do;
If once it should fail it would sure to entail
Disaster wide-spread and much suffering too.

On yonder plantation the hard toiling slave

Allowed a few moments can crack up his 'Lunch;'
The hunter afar with wild nature at war
'Tea,' 'Coffee,' or 'Osborne' can quietly munch.

Thus, then, this large firm all earth's races supply
With 'Albert,' with 'Brighton,' with 'Bath' and 'Cheapside,'
'Fancy Rout,' 'Macaroon' and the sweet 'Demi Lune'
And dear 'Littlefolk' and the 'Household' beside.

'Jamaica,' 'Pearl,' 'Button Nuts,' 'Honey Drops,'
'Maziena,' 'Empire,' 'Combination' and 'Queen;'
'Milk,' 'Camp,' 'Ratafias,' 'Captain,' Cuddy' and 'Cheese,'
'Rich Travellers,' 'Riviera,' 'Picnic,' 'Madeline.'

'Nonpareil,' 'German Rusks' and 'Caricature,'
'Digestive,' 'Colonial,' 'Nonsuch' and 'Savoy,'
'Filbert,' 'Diadem,' and the neat little 'Gem,'
'Snowflake,' 'Smyrna,' 'Social,' 'Swiss,' 'Toast,' 'Cracknell Toy.'

'Caprice,' 'Abernethy,' 'Tea Rusks,' 'Almond Rings,'
'Brown College,' 'Meat Wafers,' and 'Ice Wafers' too;
'Walnut,' 'Arrowroot,' 'Universal' and 'Fruit,'
'Thin Captain,' 'Presburg,' all most sweet, fresh and new.

'Salt,' 'Sicily Nuts,' 'Water,' 'Wheaten,' 'Wheatmeal,'
'Nic Nac,' 'Kinder Garten,' the 'Oaten' and 'Roll;'
'Moss,' 'Tourist,' 'Boudour,' and a vast number more,
I have here but mentioned a half of the whole.

—J. MOSDELL: *The Village of Mortimer and other Poems*, 1891

> Mr Mosdell's day job was village carrier in Mortimer. He earns his place in
> literary history by including a record number of biscuits in a single poem.
> One could fill a volume with Huntley-and-Palmeriana, including all 44
> stanzas of Mosdell's paean. The next poem in his unslim volume is entitled
> 'The Destruction of the Tay Bridge and the Loss of a Passenger Train', but it
> would be unfair to dub him the McGonagall of Mortimer: his verses do scan,
> and in a long preface he modestly invites the reader to consider his work as
> less than poetry.

I should like to have seen with my own eyes what success the new order of things had had in getting rid of the sprawling mess with which commercialism had littered the banks of the wide stream about Reading and Caversham: certainly everything smelt too deliciously in the early night for there to be any of the old careless sordidness of so-called manufacture.

— WILLIAM MORRIS: *News from Nowhere*, 1892

This extraordinary book, set in the year 2122, dreams of a socialist utopia established after a revolution in 1952. It was prompted partly by Edward Bellamy's *Looking Backward* (1889, set in 2000); but pre-dating both we have *The Island of Anarchy* (1887), a Utopian-Dystopian tale of the late 20th century written by Elizabeth Waterhouse of Reading. Two Rivers Press issued a facsimile edition in 1997.

We went down to Reading the other day, as so many of Miss Mitford's friends have done before, to look at 'Our Village' with our own eyes, and at the cottage in which she lived for so long. A phaeton with a fast-stepping horse met us at the station and whirled us through the busy town and along the straight dusty road beyond it. As we drove along in the soft clouded sunshine I looked over the hedges on either side, and I could see fields and hedgerows and red roofs clustered here and there, while the low background of blue hills spread towards the horizon. It was an unpretentious homely prospect intercepted each minute by the detestable advertisement hoardings recommending this or that rival pill. 'Tongues in trees' indeed, in a very different sense from the exiled duke's experience! Then we come within sight of the running brook, uncontaminated as yet; the river flowing cool and swift, without quack medicines stamped upon its waters; we reach Whitley presently, with its pretty gabled hostel ...

— ANNE THACKERAY RITCHIE, introduction to Mary Russell Mitford's *Our Village*, 1893

Anne, daughter of the poet William Makepeace Thackeray, was disappointed with the hamlet of Three Mile Cross. 'Tongues in trees' is a quote from *As You Like It*.

During that day and for many days afterwards he talked of nothing but Reading Prison and it had already become for him a sort of enchanted castle of which Major Nelson was the presiding fairy. The hideous machicolated turrets were already turned into minarets, the very warders into benevolent Mamelukes and we ourselves into Paladins welcoming Coeur de Lion after his captivity ...

— Oscar Wilde in Dieppe, 1897, reported by Robert Ross, quoted in *Selected Letters of Oscar Wilde*, edited by Rupert Hart-Davis, 1979

This anecdote shows, perhaps, that despite the horrors related in *'De Profundis'* and the *'Ballad'* Wilde retained some kind of a sense of humour.

Though the capital of Berkshire, an ancient borough and market town, with two representatives in parliament, Reading seemed some years back to be fast falling into the somnolescent state into which aged agricultural towns are prone to lapse. But it has effectively roused itself and, taking advantage of its railway and other facilities, has developed its resources in a remarkable way, and is now an active centre of industry and enterprise, and by far the busiest place on the Upper Thames.

— ANON: *Up the River from Westminster to Oxford*, 1898

Hotel of Roebuck, Tilehurst station here,
For mutual aid their edifices rear,
There a bijou chalet like a hive,
Where Croesus makes believe to poorly live.
Through bare, uninteresting reaches wide,
In calm serenity we swiftly glide,
Till smoke-grimed Caversham at length appears,
Aspect of earnest industry it wears;
Steeples and towers and streets of houses rise,
And chimneys tall pollute cerulean skies:
Here the wide course trodden by many feet,
And burnt up by the sun's excessive heat,
Borders the river; here the children play,
And pass the hours of the exuberant day.
Leaving behind the manufacturing mart,
On river journey we again depart:
The woods of Holme brood on the riverside,
And paint with depth of shade the aqueous tide.

— E. DERRY: *Rhymes of Road, Rail and River*, 1899

> Derry was evidently not a local man; perhaps, passing under Caversham
> Bridge and through Caversham Lock, he took that to be the name of the
> whole conurbation.

The town in its modern form is a splendid testimony to the local spirit of
advancement, and the work of rebuilding which has been carried out with
so much activity in the older streets has produced many handsome and
tasteful structures of which the community may well be proud. In this
respect, perhaps, no English town has made more conspicuous progress,
as the result alike of public spirit and of private enterprise.

— ANON: *Men of the Period*, c1903

It cannot be said that Reading has made the most of its Thames frontage. From Caversham Bridge to the Lock the towpath is flanked by boat
builders' and engineers' yards, and looped up with the Caversham Road
by depressingly mean streets. At the lock there is a frail wooden bridge
running behind the weir – known as 'The Clappers' – which affords a
passage to Lower Caversham, an ugly suburban excrescence of Reading.
Above the weir an arm of the river sweeps round to the left, and with

its willow-lined banks offers a pleasant walk almost to Caversham Mill, which is served by this part of the river. The eyot between the weir and this fork of the river is full of opportunity for picturesque development, but it presents a forlornly neglected appearance. … beyond the mill all is desolation: the surroundings are in a state of transition from rurality to suburban formality, and the mill stream is choked and foul. Behind and beyond the lock the King's Mead – preserved as an open space – affords the town its recreation ground and bathing-place.

— ANON: *The Thames and its Story,* 1906

Reading, in spite of its undoubted features of interest, in spite of its ancient history, is still a manufacturing town, and as such spreads around an atmosphere which is uncongenial to true Thames lovers, who regard it as a blot.

— G. E. MITTON: *The Thames,* 1906
   Geraldine Edith Mitton became Lady Scott.

Withal, Reading is at present provincial. Though so near to London it provides for the city-dweller some of those sharp surprises that strike through the bustle of a business town. The crowds of people that on certain days of the week throng the chief streets introduce by their character an element of incongruity – they are not akin to the splendid modern shop fronts and imposing premises, are not native to the new and changing town. They smack of the country and the country town – and Reading is ceasing to be that. On the electric trams you may listen on Saturday afternoon to such talk in good provincial speech that you will fancy all the local interest centres in football, and will be certain of the existence of a keen local pride. On the same day you shall see the streets and inn-yards choked by carriers' carts from a hundred hamlets round – each moving out at evening with its heavy load of village women and their marketing behind the shabby tarpaulin flaps. On Sundays there are at least three scenes of a colouring quite provincial. There is an Italian colony in Silver Street, whose members attend mass at the Roman catholic Church. If the men are soberly clad, the women and youngsters have all the brave attire that recalls days under Southern skies. When they leave the service the Forbury is brightened by sudden gleams of gay colour – unusual in our English towns. But that is not all. There are the boys of the Blue Coat School to carry the mind back to days when English costumes were more varied and brilliant than now, and – there are the girls of the Green Girls' School.

… But the station building is not alone in its unworthiness. The stranger to Reading who depends on first impressions will be tempted to flee. Here is a magnificent open space, such as is possessed by few towns, of splendid artistic and architectural possibilities, yet expressive

of naught but dreariness and desolation. A sunken meadow in front, given over to stabling and the exercising of horses; beyond, no fine frontage, but only the gaunt backs of ugly houses, and to the left the depressing S.E. station; this is what offends the eye ranging over a space with po-tentialities for picturesque treatment almost equal to Trafalgar Square. When the Borough Council is overcome with reforming zeal, here is a work to its hand.

— *The Homeland Handbook,* 1906

Now we are drawing near to Reading. The hills have receded on the left bank; the monotonous embankment of the Great Western Railway, a piece of artificial Berkshire, hides the natural Berkshire from all eyes.

Tilehurst (it is true that it is not worth a visit) is almost as far distant as Reading; but Tilehurst station, with extensive platforms and the other appanage of a railway station, is perched close to the river. Why does it exist at all? Did the railway company at any time venture to cherish the hope that upon some future day the vicinity of Tilehurst station might blossom forth as a 'riverside resort'? If so, the gloomy rampart of their own embankment should have warned them of certain failure. Or is it possible that the importance of the station is not entirely disconnected with the presence of an unassuming bungalow across the stream, where the late general manager of the railway, one of the most genial of men, was wont to make occasional holiday? To these questions there can be no answer; but it is certain that this is a dull piece of river, and that the Thames has but little charm until Caversham Bridge has been reached

and passed. Neither, just now, will we halt to look at Caversham, unlovely suburb of Reading, nor to linger in Reading itself.

For Reading, rich in memories and in history, is poor in relics and in beauty. Most of it looks as bare and newly baked as one of the biscuits of Reading fame, and the one tolerable thing seen as you pass in the train is to be found in the flashing bands and beds of colour from Messrs Suttons's nursery grounds. Nothing, or next to nothing, is gained by entering the town; for reading may be accomplished elsewhere and there is little to see. ... So let us away downstream to-day, leaving the ugliness and the prosperity of modern Reading behind with such speed as may be vouchsafed by breeze, or oars, or throbbing engine.

— J. E. VINCENT: *Highways and Byways in Berkshire,* 1906

It has become the only assize town in Berkshire, with gaol of course; it is a great agricultural market, one of the most important in England perhaps; it is a meeting-place of three railways; it is the centre of the largest biscuit manufactory in the world, that of Messrs Huntley and Palmer; the greatest seed-growing establishment of England, that of Messrs Sutton & Sons, has its headquarters at Reading; it has barracks, breweries, malt-houses. All these involve, not perhaps of necessity but as a fact, the possession by Reading of a great number of buildings distinguished by their size and by their uncompromising ugliness, and of endless streets of plain and staring red-brick houses, many of them with new slate roofs. In fact, like 'Maggie' in a recent play by Mr Barrie, if unlike her who took the part when it was first presented, Reading is useful, very useful, but it has no 'charm' … speaking generally, it is wise not to land at Reading in search of objects of interest – they are few and far between. The general aspect of the town is commonplace in the extreme; and the only strong inducement to stay at Reading a moment longer than one must, usually quite a long time if it is desired to make a through journey by the Great Western or either of the other railways, is to be found in the museum.

—J. E. VINCENT: *The Story of the Thames,* 1909

Very little of the old town remains and the new commercial buildings are depressing when they are not actually unpleasant to the eye. Over the suburbs there has spread a red rash of buildings, mostly compounded of vulgar vagaries. It's not too much to say that Reading serves as a compendium of what to avoid.

—*Country Life,* 1909

… it was in the course of one of those Easter walks I have spoken of, and the way was through Reading and by Three Mile Cross and Swallowfield. On this occasion I conceived a dislike to Reading which I have never quite got over, for it seemed an unconscionably big place for two slow pedestrians to leave behind. Worse still, when we did leave it we found that Reading would not leave us. It was like a stupendous octopus in red brick which threw out tentacles, miles and miles long in various directions – little rows and single and double cottages and villas, all in red, red brick and its dreary accompaniment, the everlasting hard slate roof. These square red brick boxes with sloping slate tops are built as close as possible to the public road, so that the passers-by by looking in at the windows may see the whole interior – wall-

papers, furniture and oftentimes the dull expressionless face of the woman of the house, staring back at you out of her shallow blue eyes.

— W. H. HUDSON: *Afoot in England,* 1909
Hudson was an American-born naturalist.

I undertook one of the most banal expeditions of my life when on a morning of early March in 1909 I went from Reading by Whitley, Hartley Court, Southcot Manor, and back again by the Bath Road to Reading. It was a grey and heavy day, filled with the South-east: an alien wind, a devastation of the soul, raising dust in choking clouds. Southward out of Reading I went across the High Bridge and along Silver Street: the great road to Southampton.

Therein stand many ancient houses of the sieviers: the old basket makers; heavily eaved: now upon their lintels are scrawled in emasculate Latin the names of exiles from Italy. Beyond the ends of the little side streets on the right as you ascend you may catch glimpses of Kennet in his receding valley. But on such a day the scene is sordid, depressing; the houses continue with scarcely a break from Reading into Whitley. Worton grange, just beyond Whitley Cross, seemed worth a passing glance through its white gate and along its little avenue. But the first sparkle on the journey was the sign of a puny, crouching inn: The World Turned Upside Down; whence at last you get an open view southwest over Kennet to Sulhamstead House.

— FRED S. THACKER: *Kennet Country,* published 1932

Reading, which is well in sight from Caversham, has a bad river approach, but is an interesting old town and a most genial centre in the hunting and shooting season.

— T. H. M. HOWE: *The Thames*, 1911

Reading is *the* place for second-hands.

— WILFRED OWEN, C1912, quoted in *Berkshire Old and New*, 2000
   Until 1989 William Smith's in London Street (the building now occupied by
   RISC) was the second-hand bookshop; now we have only Oxfam and Amnesty.
   Owen, perhaps the greatest World War I poet, lived briefly at Dunsden and
   studied botany and Latin at Reading's proto-university.

My companion was filled with disgust to think we were going to Reading. 'They are making some new tram lines, and the lodging-houses are full of navvies', he explained. … Reading being so large a town, it did not take me long to find lodgings. The first coffee house I went into and applied for a bed was glad enough to take my money. The landlady and her daughter – I could see no sign of a man – approved of my appearance at once and judged me to be quite clean and harmless.

— W. H. DAVIES: *Poet's Pilgrimage*, 1912 (published 1918)
   Davies, the Welsh poet and author of *The Autobiography of a Super-Tramp*
   was walking (mostly) from Carmarthen to Maidenhead – with an artificial leg
   – in 1912, according to internal evidence in his text. But the anecdote about

Reading and navvies, which supposedly occurred in Newbury, had already appeared in 'The Tramp', a literary walkers' magazine, in March 1910 – this time set in Wallingford; and Reading did re-lay some of its tramlines in 1909. At all events, by the time of the 'pilgrimage' Davies was a recognised writer and no longer a professional tramp. In another book he recalled a week's reading in the Free Library at Reading which he thought 'the best week's enjoyment he ever had'.

Reading is a progressive town, a busy modern place, that fills the world with biscuits, that sends its seeds into all countries, that has iron-works and printing works and tin-works, and is gay and prosperous except in war-time. It pulls down its old houses and builds greater. One of the last, which called itself Walsingham House, after Queen Elizabeth's minister, an old half-timbered structure with charming old plaster ceilings, at the corner of Minster Street and Broad Street, disappeared a few years ago. We did our best to save it, but business and modern utilitarianism were too much for us.

— P. H. DITCHFIELD: *Byways in Berkshire and the Cotswolds*, 1920
    A pre-Civic Society campaign.

In spite of the depreciatory remarks made by those who have never really taken the trouble to acquaint themselves with the merits of the place, Reading is an interesting, prosperous and pleasant town.

Even its industries 'lean to virtue's side'. For wonderful displays of floral colour, and for the production of wholesome dainties much in demand by boating and picnic parties, it is in a class by itself.

— Burrow's *Guide to the Thames Valley*, 1920

Sonning is succeeded by Reading, the county town and the largest in the county of Berkshire. It is ambitious, self-respecting, well-managed, and, what is very unusual in a town of this kind in the southern counties, very busy and prosperous. ... The town does justice to its opportunities, and has good cause to be proud of itself. It numbered at the last census (including parts of Caversham under the Act of 1911) over 80,000 persons. Few towns of that size have such ample spaces for recreation at their very gates, and the wide flats by the river and the beauties of Mapledurham and Sonning near by are fully appreciated.

— G. E. MITTON: *Buckinghamshire and Berkshire*, 1920

Reading is without doubt the most disappointing town in the whole of the Thames valley. It has had such a full share of history, far more than other equally famous towns; has been favoured by the reigning monarch of the land through many centuries; has taken sides in internal strife and felt the tide of war surging round its gates; it has counted for so much in the life of England that one feels almost a sense of loss in finding it just a commonplace manufacturing town, with not a semblance of any of its former glory.

... Now Reading passes its days independent, almost unconscious, of the past, with its glory and its tragedy. Nor does the river any more enter into its calculations. To Reading has come the railway; and the railway has made the town what it is – an increasingly important manufacturing town and railway junction, and a ready centre for the rich agricultural land round about it; a hive of industry, with foundries, workshops, big commercial buildings, and a University College; with churches, chapels, picture-palaces, and fast-moving electric-tramcars, clanging their way along streets thronged with busy, hurrying people – in short, a typical, clean, modern industrial town, with nothing very attractive about it, but on the other hand nothing to repel or disgust.

— WALTER HIGGINS: *Father Thanes*, c1920

Continuing up stream and threading many a lovely reach (but leaving Henley, with its beauties and horrors, to the biographer of Oxfordshire), Reading soon thrusts its bustling and, aesthetically speaking, offensive presence upon the traveller. No one of temperate views and even a modest standard of taste would recommend Reading as an art centre or as picturesque in itself. Its biscuits are good and no doubt it is a model community, as modern communities go, but industrialism has its stranglehold on the town, and there is far too high a proportion of what some call suburbs and others slums. Even the fragmentary remains of its once great and glorious abbey are utterly uninteresting and uninviting. But if civic memories are a greater inheritance than fine buildings, Reading has every reason to rejoice. For centuries she played a part, and a telling part, in that queer jumble of more or less incongruous happenings which we call history.

— WALTER HUTCHINSON: *Britain Beautiful*, 1924

Beyond Mapledurham the river joins the railway and the road in a race to Reading. Reading does not repay the race, and the river for some time is flat and sulky. I am not going to extol the beauties of Reading in these pages. It is an ugly town dominated by biscuits, seeds, the gaol, and a statue of Mr Palmer with bronze top-hat and umbrella, in a long bronze coat and baggy trousers. Reading has, of course, compensations, but visitors who cannot stay to find them will have a sorry time. If you do not mind an ugly building, Reading Museum has fascinating models of the Roman town of Silchester, which is itself not too far away for an afternoon's excursion. If you do not mind a stiff climb, Reading has an interesting school, in pleasant grounds; also a College soon to become a University, with some of the best teachers in the kingdom. If you do not mind undergoing an operation Reading has the most hospitable nursing-home in the world. But all these things are hidden from the casual traveller. Reading's compensations are for him overwhelmed with intolerable brick. It is, and one cannot avoid the fact, an ugly town. I do not envy Reading people Reading – save as a centre for the country round it.

It is astonishing that so little of the Reading known to history should have survived into our own time. Prosperity swamped it in brick, decorated it with the ephemeral gaudiness of advertisements, and there is hardly enough of the old town left to prove its existence before the nineteenth century. ... Reading is not exciting, I repeat. The Kennet, lovely river above Reading, takes a deathly slump here; the Thames is bored; the roads are bricked in. The engines of the railway puff in livelily; but they are going to puff out again very soon.

—F. V. MORLEY: *River Thames*, 1926

The Palmer statue, by George Simonds, was originally set up in Broad Street in 1891. As John Betjeman once said, ' trousers have been ever the bane of sculptors'.

Reading is a prosperous, well-kept and singularly unlovely manufacturing town of some 82,000 inhabitants – with clanging trams, excellent shops, and a statue of the late Mr Palmer in a frock-coat and tall hat – where neither the boating-man nor the tourist in search of beauty will be disposed to tarry overlong.

—C. FOX SMITH: *Little Guide to the Thames*, 1931

It is not until the Danish visitations, from the year 787 downwards, that there is any written history of this town that looks so modern and so banal as you toil up its slope of bricks and pavements from the river to the station after a hard day's sculling down through Wallingford or up from Marlow and Henley.

— FRED S. THACKER: *Kennet Country*, 1932

> It is not clear where Thacker got the year 787 from: 870 is the usually accepted starting point for Reading's recorded history.

… here is a small incident which occurred at CAVERSHAM one morning towards the end of May (this year, 1932) when an elderly minister curtly informed me at sight that when he wanted a book he goes to the bookseller, or, in other words, he doesn't buy from the door, although he didn't say that. There is nothing down for any day in May for the Reading area – Caversham being a large suburb of that town – so the visit was quite abortive, fruitless and futile. Was I guided to Reading that day? Do I pray as to where I should go? The answer to the first question is that if I was, there was no point in being so, for, as I said, although I worded it differently, the visit was completely barren; I was beating the air; it was totally ineffective … I told the minister that he couldn't get mine at the booksellers, because they won't have them – which certainly didn't improve matters, for that might have given the impression that they were rubbish.

— H. F. WOOD: *All Over Britain with the Author*, published 1957

> Wood, a railway clerk, published a series of religious tracts and spent all his holidays for many years travelling the country (using his free pass on the trains) trying to sell them on doorsteps. The oddest thing about this odd man and his odd book is that in 1928 he had stopped worshipping God and evangelizing: selling the tracts was henceforth just a hobby.

Between Reading and the cedar-crested bluff of Burghfield Hill, the main gateway of the pine woods, is a flat plain, pleasant enough from above and a distance, but with only the road, and that an indirect one, by which to cross it. Twenty years ago, when one could step from town to country in a few minutes, and when a trip to Reading from only five miles away was for most country folk more exciting and nearly as costly as the modern 'run up to London', I knew and loved every inch of that road, then a dusty lane foaming with sheep's parsley, through the level fields,

past the enigmatic leer of the 'Cunning Man', with a hop, skip and jump over the Kennet, canal and railway to a sedately comely Bath Road. But now Reading has found it and seems to be creeping steadily and horribly along it, sending its uglier architectural germs to infect the country ahead, and turning the forest gateway into a mere suburb. Dreadful villa diseases have scarred Burghfield Common above Burghfield Hill, and Mortimer Common nearby has an incurable rash of the worst type. Berkshire clears Bucklebury Common of gypsies and rubbish tips, and lets builders loose on Burghfield and Mortimer Commons. It is a stupid business; we spend an immense amount of money and energy preening our official Beauty Spots and allow the unofficial but not less beautiful places to be destroyed.

—J. R. A. HOCKIN: *On Foot in Berkshire*, 1934

The Burghfield Road is still dusty, thanks to the constant stream of lorries. The Cunning Man's sign leers no longer; he is now just a jolly jester, who is perhaps laughing at the ridiculous thatched pastiche of a building that replaced an unpretentious 1930s roadhouse in about 2000.

The central streets are broad and handsome, with good shops and public buildings, and some of the suburbs are pleasant, but the continually-growing wilderness of small red-brick houses has quite destroyed the picturesqueness of the town as a whole.

—F. G. BRABANT & H. A. PIEHLER: *Little Guide to Berkshire*, 1934

It is near enough to London to seem restful and even unimportant by comparison. Neither the factories nor the wealth of Reading intrude; there is none (or very little) of the hubbub usual to a prosperous town. Still, Reading is more than a prosperous town; it is one of the wealthiest in England, though it seemed surprised when I told it so. From whichever direction you enter Reading, Reading looks wealthy. Great stores and prosperous-looking shops line the wide streets. Little can demonstrate better the state of Reading's industry than the town's unemployment figures. To-day there are only 2,090 insured workers idle, almost a record low figure in a population of 100,000. Even in the height of the 1931 depression the figure was only 2,520. Perhaps its happy and healthy situation has bred contentment among its inhabitants.

— *Daily Sketch*, 1936

Caversham, just below, is Reading's well-to-do residential suburb. Reading as a go-ahead industrial town – rather grimly so for the South country – is awful in bits, but why anyone should prefer to live at Caversham I cannot think. A spiritual slum, full of the worst kind of mental squalor. Rows of pretentiously bad houses stand each in too much ground to be neighbourly, and not enough to give privacy. Everywhere, in the more prosperous streets, is the feeling that appearances are being kept up by gallant and unrewarding effort, on money that could give the owners a riotous good time in a genuine Victorian villa, instead of a pseudo-timbered neo-Georgian mansion, for which it is not quite enough. In the smaller roads, behind well-laundered net curtains, women's lives are sacrificed to the semi-detached gods – keeping one servant contented without enough assistance, and the children from playing with the noisy ones down the road. Anything – any irreparable waste of youth and interest and years unfilled with human warmth – seems to be preferable,

in Caversham, to the haunting dread of slipping back socially. Real slums leave me unmoved compared with the little prison houses built of the indomitable snobbery of bored and lonely people. I am slipshod enough to know that in a real slum I could enjoy, now and then, a row with the woman next door, before a communal audience, about what I would do to her Alice if she hit my Freddie again; and a lending of saucepans and infallible remedies in between. Certainly, as a child, I should greatly have preferred playing with dead kittens and half bricks in a crowd to wondering what I could find to do with myself, alone in a small suburban garden. And child or adult there is nowhere in England – judging unfairly, no doubt, from four visits as brief as they could be made – where I would not choose to live, in the hope of keeping some remnant of soul alive, rather than Caversham. The unemployed areas are ghastly, but they are positively so. This is not; it is negatively dreary.

Reading has its good side. Apart from the congenial curl-paper-and-jugs-of-stout reality of its poorer quarters, it has the spirit which makes the Working Men's Regatta such fun.

— E. ARNOT ROBERTSON: *Thames Portrait*, 1937
Robertson was a novelist and film critic. Was there some personal vendetta that prompted this attack on Caversham? Whence the Campaign for Real Slums?

Unfortunately, Thames Parade, as this piece of towpath is locally named, came to an end all too soon, and suddenly the town of Reading, with a gasometer near the river, burst upon our view as we emerged from the wood, and the shock was most unpleasant. Again to quote Sadler, the Sonning lock-keeper and poet:

From hence the town of Reading
Is just one field across
Mongst other things so widely known
For biscuits, seeds and sauce.

Reading certainly has gasworks, biscuit and sauce factories, a seed emporium, and a railway too near the river; also, it is frankly ugly as a whole. In just one hundred years the population has increased from sixteen thousand to one hundred thousand. Yet one may not treat the place with contumely, for it is the county town of Berkshire, and has a good deal of interesting history attached to it.

— E. K. W. RYAN: *The Thames from the Towpath*, 1938
James Sadler kept Sonning Lock from 1845 to 1885, and was also a noted rose-grower and beekeeper.

People avoid Reading but even the streets of terracotta shops and houses in the centre of town have a good deal to be said for them when you know them in different lights. A setting sun with a slight evening mist, or a damp day during open weather in February or March gives them an air that separates Reading in character from every other south country town. The washable weather-resisting surface that will hardly change with centuries of wear, changes its look constantly with the different lights of different days, and has plenty of delights to satisfy an unprejudiced eye.
— John Piper, c1939, quoted in *Piper's Places*, 1983

It has been called one of the best-looking of all our industrial towns, and certain it is that the industry that has made it has not spoiled it. The things it makes are pleasant enough or even beautiful, for its seeds cover the earth with beauty and its biscuits are everywhere. It has wide streets and green spaces, two rivers, and two railways. Its people can get anywhere easily ...

But it is of a fine modern town that we think when we think of Reading; its old ways are not thrust upon us but must be found. Its Castle Hill is a street to see a thousand times, superb, a sloping and curving thoroughfare with fine houses, white terraces, creeper-covered fronts, a big low house which was once the first coaching inn coming from Bath; and the hill commands a noble landscape. Bath Road is a glorious boulevard with houses set back in trees. The riverside promenade is beautifully laid out for a mile above Caversham Bridge – Caversham, like Tilehurst and Earley, is being swallowed up by this growing town so happily placed at the meeting of the Kennet and the Thames. Reading Bridge was one

of the most wonderful of our modern bridges when built soon after the war, its great concrete arch (spanning 60 yards) having no rival in the country. ... If Reading is to be counted as one of the pleasantest of all the towns of England, it must be reckoned also among the towns most appreciative of their natural good fortune and their social

opportunities. In the last few years it has set up its own electricity supply, has introduced the trolley-bus in place of the tram, and has greatly developed the aeroplane industry at Woodley. As an industrial town Reading has few rivals for cleanliness, attractiveness, and the general regard for the preservation of its amenities.
— Arthur Mee's *Berkshire*, 1939

After Mapledurham the face of the country is blemished by the marks of man, and if one cannot navigate that stretch of river by night the best alternative is a mild inebriation. I was unable to manage either, but I had

the good fortune to synchronize my arrival in Reading with a river-steamer, and to watch the final acrobatics of four boys who had run a parallel course for several miles along the tow-path.

Their exhibition was the nearest that I have come across, in England, to that of the diving boys and other strange performers that one sees in foreign parts. The four youngsters trotted along the tow-path as lightly as terriers on their private excursions. Suddenly one of them would let out a war-whoop. The next moment he would be executing a hand-stand on the shoulders of an accomplice, or balancing on his own head on a gate-post. After this, quite unconcernedly, he would break back into that easy trot which seemed to be his normal form of locomotion. A few minutes later one of the others would display – then they would all combine in a knock-about turn. In between these diversions their pace on the tow-path never slackened. Breath seemed unnecessary to them

When they reached the sanctified ground of the riverside park, their exhilaration and abandon increased, and they behaved with all the effrontery of merry andrews at a carnival, turning cartwheels among the astonished visitors, somersaulting over partly occupied seats, dancing on their hands, and performing other buffooneries. It was all as fresh and irresponsible as a ballet, and it happened in Reading. They collected no more than they deserved.

— ROBERT GIBBINGS: *Sweet Thames Run Softly,* 1940

> Soon after World War II Reading formed a link with the German city of Düsseldorf, which happened to have a tradition of young street acrobats dating, supposedly, from 1678; this fact is celebrated by a sculpture by Brian Slack outside Reading's Civic Centre. Gibbings, best known as a wood engraver, had local connexions: in 1924 he founded the Golden Cockerel Press at Waltham St Lawrence, and in 1936 became senior lecturer in typography, book production and engraving at Reading University.

Thinking of beer brings me to Simonds, the Reading brewers. The hopleaf is their trade-mark and though many people allege that beer is now only 'chemic' I've seen hundreds of huge bales of hops in Simonds' brewery which are teamed into the brew. The hops have lost their spongy thickness, and are as thin as oak leaves, but there's all the flavour there. When you put one into your mouth you experience another of life's little sublimities. There is an intoxication in burying your hands in a bale of hops, pulling them out filled with the glorious green things, and letting them slither through your fingers and fall in fairy green flakes back into the bale.

... Reading is also known for its two 'S's, – Sauce and Seeds. I only know that an old gentleman told me that Cocks's sauce had been famed the country over for more than a century. Sutton's, the seed firm, is better known. Whenever I had a five-bob trip to London the train passed the huge area of Sutton's blooms. I thought I was in Holland for colour. There were squares and oblongs of reds, blues, whites and yellows. No one can fail to gaze at the thousands of acres.

... Reading strikes me as being a good big town that is fortunately incapable of becoming a city, and is unfortunately becoming cinema-minded. Its suburbs are growing, and mostly into a blaze of red bricks. Some of the older suburbs are very pleasing. Fortune and nature have been kind to it, for it is unusual for towns of its size to have blown into them such great food as the pure air that comes from the Berkshire downs; or for the town to have so many miles of green land around it, such happy and useful rivers and canals and be so far from and yet so conveniently near to London.

— JACK HILTON: *English Ways,* 1940

Hilton was walking from Rochdale to Plymouth. Reading has made several bids for city status, but they are invariably rejected – probably because the Council presumptuously jumps the gun by putting 'City Centre' on the front of its buses.

Away from Caversham heights, lower horizons and a level riverside make the borders of the town of Reading. Fresh from our progress through perhaps the most beautiful scenes on the Thames we determined to enter Reading, if only to even up the impressions by the introduction of contrast. We had heard things said about Reading. The word 'horrid' often figured in descriptive phrases relating to this town. One of our books of reference displayed in capitals, 'DULL READING'. Another one concentrated on biscuits, seeds and sauce. Then the matter of a statue had been mentioned to us, complete with frock coat, top hat, unfolded umbrella, and no creases in the trousers. Our informant on this subject did not

consider the work of art in question suitable for anywhere but Reading, at the same time adding statements in general agreement with the capital letters in the reference book. For these reasons the town clearly ought to be investigated, either to prove or disprove malignant accusations, and to demonstrate the true or false meaning of adjectives and their proper application.

Thus prepared, we ascended and stood on the bridge at Caversham. Pretty quickly deciding that, for an introduction to the county town of Berkshire, the structure might have been much worse, and yet a good deal better, as it would have been if built years ago, before artistry and taste slipped down somewhat badly. ... Advancing through a maze of red bricks, under tunnels with railway lines overhead, and skirting station platforms, we eventually reached a prospect fair with sidings, factories and gasometers. 'Ah', said Anthony, while taking in the view and evidently remembering Oxford, 'I think it must be somewhere about here.'

Along the dingy banks of the river Kennet, not far from the confluence with the Thames, all sorts of picturesque bits, though rather dirty, revealed plenty of painter's subjects of a Whistler flavour. In King's Road, beyond the great home of biscuits, and elsewhere too, the regency houses exhibited that mood of architecture quite notably. Away in the opposite direction various old houses suggested just the setting for days gone by when the Flying machines and the mails, swinging along the Bath Road after changing horses at the George, speeded westward carrying Fanny Burney, Mrs Thrale, all the fashion, and figures of the peopled past, to the beautiful town of the waters. One white house, which we rambled all over and thought of buying – but one cannot possess houses everywhere – might have fitted Mr Pickwick exactly. We pictured him bulging out of the big fat bow-window waving to the coach passing along with Pecksniff and his daughters inside, muddled up in the straw with Jonas Chuzzlewit and his father snoring. The centre of the town had much life, and even gaiety flitting about; lots of people, and lots of shops. Very good shops, too. Londoners could think of home; eat with Mr Stewart of Bond Street,

or buy nice things from Mr Peter Jones, sent down from Sloane Square for local consumption. Altogether, dull Reading of the capital letters looked quite brilliant.

The sight of Huntley and Palmer's huge frontage, and feelings of hunger, agitated thoughts of biscuits. A shop close at hand, exhibiting the words 'Broken Biscuits' inscribed on a card, introduced an ample display of boxes and tins filled with the local and battered commodity. Four shillings would secure a huge bulk, tin included, while for sixpence any single individual might go a buster. As a tin looked too large for pilgrims to pilot up and down the Thames, we acquired a large full bag for one shilling, containing nearly enough food to feed the five thousand. Gleeful in obtaining something for almost nothing, as human beings feel when they think they have secured a bargain, we returned to the river once more to seek out a quiet spot where the contents of the bag might be examined and securely eaten. Screened by willow trees, and secure behind the moat formed by the river, we settled down to probe the mysteries of Huntley and Palmer's making. This diversion brought thrills at least equal to those experienced in solving crossword or jigsaw puzzles. In picking out unexpected particulars from the general mass, the element of surprise never failed. The selection was choice and varied; not all the biscuits were broken. The miniature cave of delight, well upholding the

world-wide reputation of its creators, had all the magic of an Arabian Night's entertainment. Frances discovered little round macaroon things which she said cost no end a pound in the region of Brompton Road or Piccadilly, and Anthony, a mere infant, revelled in bits of animals and birds made for juvenile consumption.

— S. R. JONES: *Thames Triumphant*, 1943

A pleasing collection of cottages border the way here – the little village of Calcot Row. Then comes the best scenery of the day – so far it has been uninteresting. Trees come back again near the road, stately and fine and friendly. So for two miles into the suburbs, a magnificent park stretches on the left sloping up to higher ground, and finally one enters between superior houses set in lawns and gardens into the very substantial looking town.

It takes fully an hour to find lodging for the night. Then I succeed in an hotel that no impartial and sober man would call inviting; but as necessity is the mother of other things beside invention – compromise has it. Supper consists of cold meat that long ago was part of a lamb, followed by cold prunes and cold comfort, all with their respective appurtenances!

— ARTHUR ARNOLD: *A Winding Trail*, 1943

Arnold was walking from Milford Haven to Sheerness. Prospect Park and its mansion survive, but most of the superior houses along the Bath Road have been replaced by flats.

Reading is an ancient town. A castle, holy relics, a nunnery, duelling knights – all these can be found in its history. But what one notices today are its trams, its factories and its greyhound races, and the only joyful notes are contributed by the kindergarten beside the railway lines, and the flower-beds whose bright colours blaze out under the dark chimneys of the adjacent biscuit factory. The dog-races and the cinema are the common diversions of any industrial town; but Reading also boasts a repertory theatre and the best second-hand bookshops of all Thames-side towns – excepting Oxford.

— *La Grande Bretagne*, 1947 (editor's translation)
 The trams had been replaced by trolleybuses in 1936.

Angst begins at Reading.
— CYRIL CONNOLLY: *The Unquiet Grave*, 1948

Like many other industrial communities, it appears at its worst from the railway-line, but its natural surroundings are pleasing, and it might be rendered much more attractive if full use were made of the comparatively new art or science of town-planning.

— MARTIN BRIGGS: *Down the Thames*, 1949

This, the capital of the county, is a much-maligned town. Too many people see it only from the railway and dismiss it as a modern place as they glide past a china orchard of electric transformers, the gay colours of Sutton's seed beds, Huntley and Palmer's biscuit factory and the castellated red-brick gaol (1833) where Oscar Wilde languished. Motorists horrified by the hideous villadom along the road from London after Waterer's Floral Mile, infuriated by the long traffic wait at the Grecian Cemetery gates (H. Briant, 1842) with Doric chapels among the tombs, are too upset to notice the noble lines of late Georgian terraces along the London Road. They only recover in time to see the curious curve of villas on the by-pass to the Bath Road. Even shoppers along Broad Street and Oxford Road, now the main shopping streets of the town, can hardly fail to be startled by McIlroy's fantastic building designed at the beginning of this century by Mr Frank Morris, an affair of stepped gables and corbelled balconies in red and yellow glazed bricks and granite all resting, apparently, on two tall storeys of plate glass.

… Thus with its railwayside industrialism, its miles of hard red suburbs and the weird commercial architecture at its centre, Reading at superficial glance seems hideous. Yet the space between the London Road on the south and the railway on the north is full of decent architecture as befits the capital of a county. It is mostly Georgian and early Victorian. No town in the south of England hides its attractions more successfully from the visitor.

— JOHN BETJEMAN AND JOHN PIPER: *Murray's Berkshire Architectural Guide*, 1949
> The gaol was actually built in 1843; the cemetery chapels have gone;
> McIlroy's, once dubbed Reading's Crystal Palace, happily survives, though the
> plate glass trick has been spoilt by recent refenestration.

Reading, the county town of Berks, is a thriving modern manufacturing town with far-spreading suburbs. Once noted for its clothing industry, which flourished during the Middle Ages, it is now famous for beer, seeds and biscuits. … The streets of the main shopping area are aggressively modern.

— R. L. P. JOWITT: *The Penguin Guide to Berkshire and Oxfordshire*, 1950
> This is the earliest hint that I have found of the 'Three Bs' tag.

Then suddenly the river magic is shattered. Ahead a great power station rears up from a vacant flat of waste land – a clear case for screening by trees. Now we are in for nearly three miles of squalor, at least on the Berkshire side – the gas works, railway sidings, unfeeling walls of grimy machine-made bricks, rusting corrugated iron roofs, chaos of overhead wires all set amidst tufts of sooty, half-dead grass while in the distance rise the factory chimneys above the grey slate roofs of READING ...

— ERIC DE MARÉ: *Time on the Thames,* 1952

For myself, I think that no town should be so big that one cannot walk across it and out of it in a morning. Reading pleases me in this respect. It is not big enough to enslave its people, to offer them urban apathy and delirium in place of dignity. Not yet. But I see signs of encroachment on the wooded clearing. I hear rumours of building on the park opposite my house, of roads being cut through, of buses and Woolworths and Odeons. With something approaching dismay I anticipate by writing 'Reading, sw1' on my letter paper ...

— Alan Wykes in *Reading Review,* 1953

It takes six months for anything new to catch on in Reading. Housewives prefer to wait until a friend has tried it out first – and that is how I was introduced to the plastic bucket. They have been on sale in Reading for some time now, but many people do not realise what a bargain they are.

— *Coronation Reading,* 1953

Blake's Lock is rarely used, but it is kept in excellent order and its paint was as bright as the fine show of daffodils along its margins when we passed. The lock-keeper at first thought we had come the wrong way by mistake, but we assured him that Newbury was our destination. He

seemed doubtful, but did not like to discourage us. Beyond Blake's the Kennet is flanked by a street almost deserted of traffic, with a long row of small cottages and inns of no great architectural merit but having a most attractive effect. The scene was very like the canalside streets of any small Dutch town. The only great difference lay in the absence of boats – though a derelict narrowboat lay half submerged further ahead.

— ROGER PILKINGTON: *Thames Waters*, 1956

Through traffic from Reading to Bath on the Kennet and Avon ceased in 1951 and recommenced in 1990.

At the back of the prison were a little park and some public gardens. Children were bowling hoops around the boarded-up bandstand where the Temperance Brass Band played on summer Sunday evenings. A few people were walking briskly along the gravel paths, between wind-raked evergreens. These paths wound up towards a shrubbery on a small hill where there was a great cast-iron statue of a lion, a landmark for miles. Some boys were now walking round it, looking up at its huge testicles and sniggering.

This hateful town! thought Angel.

— ELIZABETH TAYLOR: *Angel*, 1957

The author, a native of Reading, renames it 'Norley' and somewhat rearranges the Forbury Gardens.

Today Reading is too near London for its position to have the same significance; the river has ceased to bear trade, and cars on the road and expresses on the rail pass it by without halting, but it is still a junction of road and rail, and the volume of traffic that pours through the main streets and the General (Western Region) station by day and night is immense.

— DAVID KNOWLES: *The Monastic Order in England: a History of its Development*, 1963

Knowles was commenting on my very first quote from William of Malmesbury.

Towards Reading factories as large as villages interrupt a scenery that Corot might have painted, where many fields have been lost to water-filled gravel pits. The Kennet ceases to be a fly-fisherman's stream to become a coarse-fisherman's river, where in recent years bream have become more populous than roach, while tench and pike are caught in the gravel pits.

Reading was a country town before it became an industrial one, and grew fat on the corn-land of its countryside, for though English wheat does not make the best bread it bakes the best biscuits. The Thames-side town grew up on the banks of the Kennet where the Normans built an abbey of flint on the river bank. Few abbeys can have stood in a more sublime setting, overlooking a stream so transparent that every fish was visible where the water meadows stretched towards the wider Thames – a landscape that inspired 'Summer is icumen in'. This first lyric and part-song in our language, written in local dialect by a monk of Reading Abbey, is a blossom on the grafted stock from which our speech is pruned, and sings the natural music of the English tongue when harnessed to song. The complex yet simple gaiety of this rhyming tune outsoars its quaintness on the printed page, as its spontaneous happiness has outlived the tragedy of the walls that first listened to its harmony.

— **BRIAN WATERS**: *Thirteen Rivers to the Thames*, 1964

> For a more accurate account of 'Sumer is icumen in', aka the Reading Rota, see the illustrated edition published by Two Rivers in 2006. Its launch party, in the Abbey ruins, was a rare and moving occasion: a large crowd sang a 750-year-old piece of music in the (probable) place of its composition.

Reading, Berkshire, where I live (though I am not a Readingensian) is an overcrowded industrial town of, at the time of writing, some hundred and twenty-five thousand people. The building of the M4 motorway has brought London within a possible forty minutes' fast driving – always assuming you can extricate yourself from the traffic muddles of the town centre and strike the motorway before you are shrivelled to a bunch of frustrations – and this possibility has encouraged a great many industrialists to hive their offices and factories off from London's great wen and attach them to Reading's smaller one; so the great and the small will soon be joined by the carcinoma of twentieth-century conurbation.

The town is administratively half-baked, artistically null, and, apart from a very few vistas of decrepit but otherwise pleasing eighteenth-century houses, architecturally hideous. (Even that enthusiastic proponent of Victorian design Mr John Betjeman is said to have blenched and asked for a restorative glass on seeing the town hall for the first time.)

— **ALAN WYKES**: *An Eye on the Thames*, 1966

> Wykes's final Betjemanian allegation is hard to believe.

For some reason Sonning is always a windy corner, as though the air itself is anxious to escape finally from the grime of Reading.

It is impossible to visit Reading, even by water, without wondering how any city can possibly contrive to be so down-at-heel and dreary. The fact is that the destruction begun by Henry VIII has been relentlessly continued by modern industry, so that what was once an abbey city in one of England's loveliest shires and at the confluence of two of her most beautiful rivers is now a sort of sprawling tip-heap, the odour of burning garbage sweetened a little with sewage, coal gas, and a back-kitchen aroma of biscuits baking.

— ROGER PILKINGTON: *Small boat on the Thames*, 1966

Meanwhile, the Thames suddenly stumbles on a state of affairs which causes one to blink and then to wince. First, a power station appears, rearing like a poisonous fungus in the waste land; after that, shunting sheds in various shades of British Railways dirt, followed by gas-works, tin huts, and factories wreathed with pylons and cables which, if they were reproduced in little, would be acclaimed as the sculpture of the year; and above the lot, a cancerous halo.

'There exists in human nature,' says Gibbon, 'a propensity to depreciate the advantages and to magnify the evils, of present times.' There does

indeed, and I have already warned myself against it, with some remarks about country life a hundred years ago; but at Reading the evils have no need to be magnified; they do it for themselves. Worse even than Oxford, this reach is not simply a blot on the landscape; it is a landscape in itself.

... Our forefathers lived amid filth, and kings went rank and stinking; but not even the lousiest of them caused, or could have conceived, the calculated squalor which infects the Thames at Reading.

Of Reading itself I shall say only this, that during the nineteenth century it suffered an acute attack of prosperity, from which it has never recovered.

— J. H. B. PEEL: *Portrait of the Thames*, 1967

Reading must be the deadliest, dullest, most boring dragsville with the powers and dignity of a County Borough and seat of a University anywhere south of Reykjavik.

— 'Bumpkin', *Village Voice* (Caversham Park Village magazine), 1968

Sonning is a pleasantly pretty village although it cannot be seen from the river and if for provisioning or other reasons you are going to go ashore in the next hour or two, then this is the place to do it if only to avoid Reading ahead. Above the lock and for a short distance to the left bank the scene is not too bad, helped as it is by the wooded hills of Holme Park, but we are soon to navigate a right-hand bend and from now on and for a long dreary pull the journey is a most unlovely one. Soon electric pylons, gasometers and a horribly plain biscuit factory are going to colour our recently acquired impression of the Thames and while somebody has obviously got to navigate it is suggested in all seriousness that the other members of the party might profitably go below, draw the curtains and forget the world outside.

And what a dreary world it is! If the industrial backcloth were not enough, and it is very bad, then the river banks themselves make it worse. It is not uncommon, even on a weekday, to see a thousand anglers, grim and grey-faced men in nondescript attire, lining the bank a standard ten feet apart for all the world like badly made but identical statues. As your boat comes abreast of them in the river and perhaps for a mile or more, you will suffer the imprecations of their wrath and even a hurled stone or two is not unlikely. They are somehow a not unfitting welcome to this dismal place and the sooner we can get beyond it the better.

— ROY CURTIS: *Thames Passport*, 1970

'So where are we going?'

'Reading, son.' My dad spoke of it as if he were talking of Shangri-La.

'Where's Reading?'

— Kenneth Branagh on moving house in 1970, in *Beginnings*, published 1989
  Older residents may remember Branagh's youthful performance in a Victorian
  melodrama at Progress Theatre.

When I first came to Reading in 1972 from Glasgow I soon realised why it was nicknamed 'Deading'. The whole town centre went to sleep in the evenings and such pubs that were in that area were dingy holes full of 'boring old farts' and served one lager and one bitter and hardly any food.

— Stephen J. Foley in the *Evening Post*, 1998
  Yes, it really was ridiculously difficult to get anything to eat in those days.

Reading, which is about the most under-rated large town in the South, still has an abundance of decent buildings, despite recent batterings, but it can ill afford to lose its focally placed Town Hall whose distinctive brick tower groups so well with the mediaeval tower, largely faced with dark Victorian flint, of St Laurence's church.

— *The Victorian Society Annual*, 1972–3
  Yes, the wonderful Town Hall really was threatened with demolition.

Reading, at first sight, is bewildering. Its approach by road from the M4 is frankly depressing, and even when reached from the river its mélange of architectural styles and apposition of buildings very different in function from each other makes for confusion in the stranger's mind. It is a town which does not hold out a very welcoming hand to the traveller, because it is not quite like anywhere else. It is as though the ancient city had been given a nervous breakdown by the changes which have come to it: industry, a university, concrete tower blocks, a multistorey car park. It has to be explored for the things which make it unique and interesting, accepting the rather sad terrace houses with their dark red brick facades, suggestive of the Midlands, and the fact that railway junctions and biscuit factories, however useful, do not make for beauty or architectural cohesion. Most of the things worth seeing in Reading (and there are many) have been in it a long time.

... In Forbury Gardens, the site of the abbey remains, is a startling war memorial in the form of an enormous lion, over seventeen feet long and sixteen tons in weight, portrayed in the act, apparently, of taking a comfortable stroll with its front legs while running with its back ones, and either chatting with a friend or giving voice to an earth-shattering roar; without more intimate knowledge of the habits of lions it is hard to tell. It is a lion worthy to take its place beside the Biggest Aspidistra in the World.

— MARY ATKINSON: *The Thames-side Book*, 1973

The extravagance begins to fade as you get closer to Reading and the dreariest section of the whole river. You get a view of the old gaol where Oscar Wilde wrote his ballad, the Huntley and Palmers factory, a solidly respectable Victorian building that one would once have described as typical of the town, and the new blocks. And the gasometer. You can see it for miles, and I have often wondered what myopic planner ever gave permission for such a structure on such a site. Reading is Britain's average town. Whenever the market research lads want to try out Brand X, they trundle it over to Reading. If it gets the thumbs-up there, then it's straight into the shops; thumbs-down, and it's back to the drawing board.

I sometimes get this awful thought: are we doomed to live in a land where everybody ends up Reading-style? Looking around at the bland drabness of the town, the awful, dull, flat anonymity, the prospect seems too hideous to contemplate.

— ANTHONY BURTON: *Back Door Britain,* 1977
  I have corrected what I take to be a misprint in this extract: the book has 'soildly' for 'solidly'.

'The total town'; 'a pleasant residential town'; 'an inland holiday resort'; 'too near London to have any life of its own'; 'a cold cancer of a town'.

— Quoted by David Cliffe in *The Stranger in Reading, an Unofficial Guide,* 1978
  Reading's third 'Stranger' book assembles five quotes that I have not used in this anthology. There must be many more awaiting discovery.

'Davis – he's a Reading University man, isn't he?' Daintry asked with what might have been a slight touch of disdain.

— GRAHAM GREENE: *The Human Factor,* 1978

The next morning my host dropped me off in Reading on his way to work and I had a cup of tea while I waited for the moleskin shop to open. Reading is not a town about which much that is flattering has been said. Understandably. There are a few good buildings, even modern ones, but the overall effect is of utter scrappiness. I found the Thames at Caversham bridge beside the Headquarters of the Thames Conservancy. I descended to the towpath and followed the river to Tilehurst.

The houses on the opposite bank were large and luxurious – Reading seemed like an aberration. For the fourth day I was following the Thames and gazing at one desirable residence after another. It seemed that most people lived thus. Reading was different – the gas holders, the litter, the awful takeaway, the traffic, the stench. Of course the bulk of the population live in the Readings of England, but it was easy, on this walk along the Thames towpath, to believe otherwise.

— ROGER JONES: *Green Road to Land's End,* 1986

Reading, it seems, is a town strangers visit only when absolutely necessary, and their reaction once here is usually to get out again as quickly as possible. Once safely outside, the town's name will crop up occasionally in their conversation, mostly as a metaphor for something unpleasant.

Reactions differ to the changing landscape of Reading. Some, lamenting the loss of Victorian charm, insist that new houses are built with the traditional multi-coloured brickware, mimicking the cast-over buildings they replace. Others regard the developing town as a canvas for the adventure of modern architecture.

Among this radical change, Reading remains an intelligent and unpretentious town to live in. Despite the popular myth, there is a lot going on here, as this guide bears testimony. A lot of people are getting a lot out of Reading, it's just that no-one makes a fuss about it.

No, Reading is not generally hailed as somewhere to spend your summer holidays. Whether your quest is for sparkling glamour or quaint charm, you can be reassured that it will not be found in Reading. The fact that people can live and enjoy living in Reading remains one of the great riddles of the universe. And yet, most Reading folk seem to like it here, and some are even downright enthusiastic about it.

—JAMES MATTHEWS: *Reading Between the Lines, the unofficial guide to Reading,*
1987

James it was who introduced me to a loose network of people who cared about Reading; his guides were a catalyst for my own writing about the town.

The old centre of Reading … is separated from the Thames by the main railway line, and the Intercity trains rushing through the station somehow symbolize the story of the town. For Reading has always been a place of transit and transiency, a halting-place on the mainline of history, often appearing in terms of a return ticket.

— MILES JEBB: *A Guide to the Thames Path*, 1988

Reading has often had less than a good press, but it has the kind of central area that is better seen on foot than from a car. If you walk about looking above the shop fronts at the buildings themselves there is much of interest.

— RICHARD LETHBRIDGE: *New Shell Guide to Oxfordshire and Berkshire*, 1988

I walk on for a mile past Tilehurst, where I meet the unkempt fringes of Reading. This reach of the maturing river has its own name, the Kentwood Deeps. Between Poplar Island and Appletree Eyot, hard under the railway line a kingfisher is released from my bank to the other as if on a tight thread drawn sharply in. There are whizzing trains, and a factory.

'Free Stonehenge 1985' counsels an old daub. This intense plea from the hippy consciousness is a clue to the nature of the remarkable assembly I am shortly to meet. A High Speed Train glints away in the western sun. There is the acrid whiff of locomotive brakebox.

I hear what sounds like the amplified summons to a phone in a factory. But it is not a factory. The town has been overtaken by an event that drives local people out in the sort of refugee convoys that clog the roads of a country when invasion is imminent. It is the Reading Rock Festival.

The first signs are young men seeking bucolic refuge in a field of cows, next to the village of tents. They wear sleeveless leather jackets and display bare arms. Some are hacking at a tree, with the uncertainty of returnees to nature.

I am to walk through this bizarre, rather menacing community on the public footpath. Will they rush at me with knives or smother me with welcomes and drag me, like a long lost friend, into their celebrations?

The trained ear can unscramble the sound of twenty 'ghetto blasters', all playing different music. Bottles without messages are bobbing in the river. I see a grinning policeman holding his boot in mock threat over the face of a recumbent fan, displaying the enforced humour obligatory on these occasions.

'We haven't seen any bands yet, we are just sort of in the water,' says a voice from the river. This is Peter Hunter, a Niagara Falls head of Pre-Raphaelite red hair tumbling down his neck. He and his party are standing in the Thames like semi-submerged oracles on this warm summer day. He offers me a bottle of Ruddles County beer, which is providing communal refreshment.

He explains how the joyous decibels will overwhelm Reading in the next few days and nights. The sound rises from the festival field, travels north across the river, bounces off the houses on the other bank and surges back to reinforce and reinvigorate the sounds that succeed it.

… I find Reading a self-sufficient place, a busy prosperous town in a region dominated by the development of the microchip. Its speciality is 'biscuits, beer and bulbs' according to the tourist brochure. It is the most unpretentious place I have yet met on the Thames.

— **GARETH HUW DAVIES**: *A Walk along the Thames Path*, 1989

The cows are still there next to Cow Lane, a few hundred metres from Reading station.

Reading? It'll be nice when it's finished.
— **ANON**, 1989, in *Catalyst* 17

Reading was a town with a charm all of its own. As we slipped under the town bridge an empty Toblerone packet landed in the boat thrown by a lad who leant over the parapet with his tongue stuck out. I said 'what's your name?!' And he shouted back: 'Nigel Layton, aged twelve, what of it, mister?'

And then by Caversham Bridge a gang of skinheads sat all over a bench, smoking and shouting and throwing things. I asked them what Reading was like and they were surprised to find someone addressing them. They were suddenly quiet as they tried to work out who was to be their spokesman. Finally, one said: 'it's got an inner ring road and an outer ring road.' And then another said: 'it's got a biscuit factory.'

— MARK WALLINGTON: *Boogie up the River*, 1989

The skinheads were wrong on two-and-a-half counts, but at least they were vaguely aware of the town's history.

Connoisseurs of urban beastliness would probably agree that Reading – the county town of Berkshire – has become one of the most unpleasant places in southern England. Reduced by economic boom and planning idiocy to a traffic-choked hell-hole studded with a display of the most mediocre office blocks and 'shopping malls' devised by contemporary architecture, it now vies with Slough for the title of most reviled town in the home counties.

Yet even Reading has its redeeming features. An outstanding fishing tackle shop, excellent game butchers and delicatessen, and a gentlemen's outfitters where the staff have tape measures around their necks and sell proper corduroy trousers, are among its civilising influences.

Until recently there was another – the second-hand and antiquarian book business incorporated in William Smith's London Street Bookshop. For 150 years or so, this has provided not only a blessed refuge for that amiable breed of timewaster, the browser, but a place of hope for the would-be purveyor of unreadable rubbish – unkindly characterised by George Orwell as 'a decayed person smelling of old breadcrumbs'.

But now the university booksellers, Blackwell & Son – who own William Smith's – have inflicted a painful blow on Reading's surprisingly large population of such souls. The bookshop has been moved to a town-centre site, and the antiquarian business has been closed.

— Tom Fort in *The Sunday Correspondent*, 1989

In 1970 Alan Wykes wrote that William Smith's 'occasionally builds up local authors to the extent of displaying a few copies of their books in the window, though not with much more than the enthusiasm of a maiden aunt displaying her underwear'. In due course Blackwells abandoned Reading altogether, but the Deli, the butcher and Jackson's happily remain.

Reading looks pretty much like any other town. There's a Timothy White's and Woolworths.

— John Peel, quoted in *Catalyst* 32, 1990

The biggest car park in Britain.

— *The Face* magazine, 1990

I actually like Reading, I really do. I find it interesting and exciting. But it's also a stupid place. When you tell people you come from Reading, they exclaim 'poor you!' When you ask them if they've ever been here, they say 'Oh well … I've been through it a couple of times on the train.' People just seem to have missed the soul of Reading.

— Eric Stanford in *Catalyst* 50, 1991

When Stanford lived in Reading he was a great champion of the town and its history. For some years he was Keeper of Art at the Museum, and a piece of his own sculpture, a memorial to Reading men of the International Brigade killed in the Spanish Civil War, stands outside the Civic Centre. A Labour – nay, positively Socialist – Councillor, he was proud to be labelled a 'loony lefty' by The Sun.

No one has visions at Reading or comes away claiming spiritual enlightenment. No one would want to: Reading offers the herbal highs, veggie burgers and crap comedians expected of festivals, but no Glastonbury-style 'sacred spaces' or Hare Krishnas.

— Gareth Cartwright: review of rock festival,
 The Guardian, 1997

Shock is the only way to describe what it is like to play on the outside of the back desks in the Barbican, the Royal Festival Hall or the Reading Hexagon. You hear no-one but yourself and the sound is pathetically small because the acoustics are dead.

— ELIZABETH ANDREWS: *Healthy Practice for Musicians*, 1997
  A warning to those who think a replacement for the Hex can be just another cheap, all-purpose, falling-between-stools theatre-cum-concert-hall.

Reading is an agricultural centre noted for the bulbs produced in its nursery gardens. Its other best-known industries are biscuit manufacture and malting and brewing, but there is much business in printing, iron foundries, engineering works, and computers. There are pottery and brickworks, together with riverside boatbuilding yards.

— *Encyclopaedia Britannica*, CD version, 1998
  One wonders what procedures encyclopedists use to update their works. This entry is little changed from the 1926 printed edition.

Robinson had moved to Reading, which is a very interesting place. There have been an unusually large number of TV documentaries made about it. 'The Family' was made in Reading, and the series about the Thames Valley Police. It also has a good art school, which has a respectability that Robinson might try to attach himself to.

— PATRICK KEILLER: *Robinson in Space*, 1999
  This book was made into a strange, actorless film: the first few minutes are set in Reading during the brief reign of Mainline's routemaster buses.

WE DON'T WANT TO END UP LIKE READING
— Headline in the *Henley Standard*, 1999

'Does Reading still smell?'
— Overheard c2000
  Not of baking or brewing; car exhaust is so permanent and ubiquitous that we don't notice it.

Nothing interesting has ever happened in Reading, with the arguable exception of Oscar Wilde's imprisonment, and there is no indication that anything interesting is going to happen there in the future, making it an ideal haven for those seeking refuge from the interesting times in which we live. This would seem to rule out the risks of terrorist atrocities, anthrax attacks, collateral damage from cruise missile strikes and unexpected coalition-building visits from Tony Blair – although international lawyers have convincingly argued that the Utopia nightclub on Pincents Lane on a Friday night constitutes a crime against humanity.

— Oliver Burkeman in *The Guardian*, 2001

As far as towns with bad presses go, Reading's cuttings file is only marginally thinner than Milton Keynes'. Eaterie-wise the reputation is unfair – whereas M. K. has little to offer beyond chain gastro-pubs, Reading has more than its fair share of quality restaurants.

— *The Guardian*, 2002

Rare praise from the national press, but a little puzzling for the date: perhaps the writer thought Shinfield was inside the Borough. But in 2008 there are several very good places in the town centre.

… Reading is now seen as a dynamic urban city undergoing a remarkable renaissance. It is a popular centre for shopping, night-time leisure, and working. More and more people want to live here, work here, and study here. When Reading is mentioned in the national media it is increasingly in a positive context; for example as a town so popular that employers are struggling to recruit.

— Reading Borough Council: *Draft Cultural Strategy*, 2002

Note the municipal mind's confusion: city or town?

Mention the town of Reading to many people and they think of Oscar Wilde's Ballad of Reading Gaol, or tell you that the town is impossible to get into by car, or that the middle has all gone and it is just a doughnut with a ring road and vast suburbs.

— MARTIN ANDREW: *Reading, a Pocket Album*, 2003

It may be shiny and new, but the whiff of boredom, wretchedness and despair reaches the nostrils and reminds one of the acrid rotten foundations.

I'm taking advantage of the ridiculous house prices and moving very shortly.

Reading is but 30 minutes from London, yet it feels like a lifetime away.

Thousands come to sit in endless traffic jams, fighting their way through the lung-busting smog.
— *Crap Towns*, 2003, in which residents were encouraged to insult the places they lived in.

Kate Winslet is a proper Reading girl: unpretentious, zero bullshit, down-to-earth, funny, and friendly.
Reflected glory – or humility – reported by Gordon McCabe on his blog, 2007.

Reading is a gloomy town with nightmarish traffic problems that affect people's wellbeing and ruin its appearance – and it's getting worse. This is the bleak picture painted by people who have sent their comments to the Reading Independent Transport Commission, according to the final analysis of responses.

— *Reading Evening Post*, February 2008.

The bleak picture was the work of a self-selecting group of citizens. Whatever Reading's problems, the demand for houses and flats remains insatiable: for some reason thousands of people still want to live here. It can't be that bad. And one can hardly argue with the Commission's final report, published on 1 July 2008, when it says:

This is a town struggling to be a city.

INDEX OF AUTHORS AND SOURCES